BREAKTHROUGH

Katalin Karikó and the mRNA Vaccine

Stephanie Sammartino McPherson

TF
CB

TWENTY-FIRST CENTURY BOOKS / MINNEAPOLIS

For my husband, Richard; our grandchildren, Kiernan, Adelaide (Addie), and Hadley; and their cousins, Joseph, Christopher, James, and Aria

Twenty-First Century Books™
An imprint of Lerner Publishing Group, Inc.
241 First Avenue North
Minneapolis, MN 55401 USA

For reading levels and more information, look up this title at www.lernerbooks.com.

Main body text set in Avenir LT Std.
Typeface provided by Adobe Systems.

Map and diagrams by Laura K. Westlund, pp. 8, 20, 23, 27, and 99.

Library of Congress Cataloging-in-Publication Data

Names: McPherson, Stephanie Sammartino, author.
Title: Breakthrough: Katalin Karikó and the mRNA vaccine / Stephanie Sammartino McPherson.
Description: Minneapolis, MN, USA: Twenty-First Century Books, [2023] | Includes bibliographical references and index. | Audience: Ages 12–18 | Audience: Grades 7–9 | Summary: "Breakthrough chronicles the life, hard work, and accomplishments of Katalin Karikó, one of the pioneering mRNA researchers whose work led to COVID-19 vaccines, depicting her as an inspirational figure for readers interested in science"—Provided by publisher.
Identifiers: LCCN 2022056204 (print) | LCCN 2022056205 (ebook) | ISBN 9798765607947 (lib. bdg.) | ISBN 9798765607954 (eb pdf)
Subjects: LCSH: Karikó, Katalin—Juvenile literature. | Biochemists—Biography—Juvenile literature. | Hungarian Americans—Biography—Juvenile literature. | mRNA vaccines—Juvenile literature. | COVID-19 vaccines—Juvenile literature.
Classification: LCC QP511.8.K37 M37 2023 (print) | LCC QP511.8.K37 (ebook) | DDC 572.092 [B]—dc23/eng/20230119

LC record available at https://lccn.loc.gov/2022056204
LC ebook record available at https://lccn.loc.gov/2022056205

Manufactured in the United States of America
1-1009091-51433-6/7/2023

Contents

INTRODUCTION

Masked and wearing a sleeveless orange blouse, sixty-five-year-old Katalin (Kati) Karikó calmly watched the needle prick her arm. Her colleague Dr. Drew Weissman, seated beside her, rolled up his sleeve for a shot too. It was December 18, 2020, and they were among the first Americans to receive a COVID-19 vaccine. As biotechnology researchers whose work helped pave the way for this vaccine, they hoped everyone would follow their example. There was no time to lose.

For most of the year, the coronavirus disease COVID-19 had been raging across the globe. It originated in China in December 2019, but by March 26, 2020, the United States was rapidly becoming its epicenter, with more than 82,000 confirmed cases and over 1,000 deaths. On November 4 the US hit a terrible milestone when, for the first time, 100,000 new cases were reported in one day. December proved even worse, with 65,000 deaths and 118,720 patients hospitalized in that month.

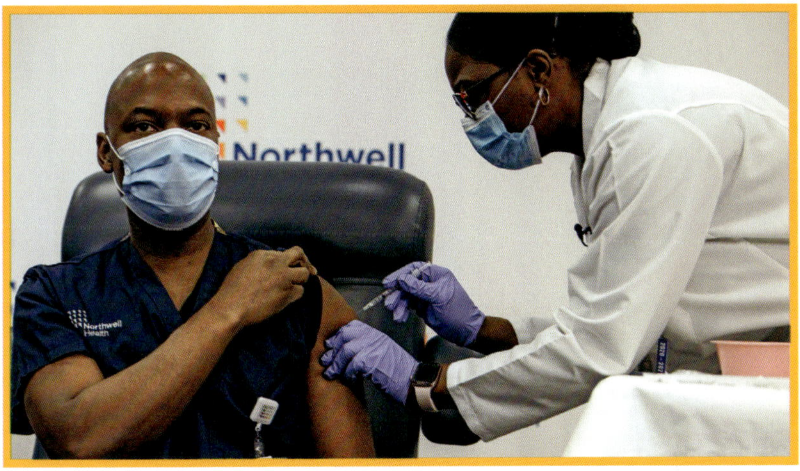

Among the first people to receive the newly approved mRNA vaccine for COVID-19, so-called frontline workers included doctors, nurses, and other health-care professionals. They worked harder than many of us can imagine to save lives and prevent the spread of the disease.

The emergency use authorization (EUA) from the Food and Drug Administration (FDA) for the Pfizer-BioNTech COVID vaccine, soon followed by an EUA for the Moderna vaccine, was the first hopeful news in a year of devastating loss and hardship. Although people around the world welcomed the lifesaving vaccinations, many were concerned about how quickly they had been developed. Normally, it takes scientists years, even decades, to produce a vaccine. The COVID vaccines had been formulated in less than a year. Some people wondered if the vaccines had been developed too quickly. Were they really safe?

The answer, Karikó knew, was a resounding yes. Perhaps more than anyone else, she realized that years of experimentation underlay the seemingly rapid success of the vaccines. Long before anyone heard of COVID, Karikó had been researching messenger ribonucleic acid (mRNA), a molecule found in all living cells. She believed the remarkable substance could be used to cure many illnesses and create more effective vaccines. For years, other scientists took little interest in what seemed to them a far-fetched prospect. But despite discouragement and lack of funding, Karikó and Weissman persisted. The biotechnology they developed based on mRNA made the rapid development of the COVID vaccines possible. Karikó and Weissman hoped that receiving their shots publicly at the University of Pennsylvania, home to their collaboration and groundbreaking work, would help allay concerns some people had about the vaccines.

When they had walked down the hallway toward the vaccination site, the chair of neurosurgery had publicly acknowledged their indispensable contribution to the vaccine. Health-care workers waiting to get their shots burst into spontaneous applause.

Karikó's eyes filled with tears. "I feel humbled and happy," she said afterward. "I am more a basic scientist, but I always wanted to do something to help patients."

Despite becoming a sudden celebrity, Karikó remains down-to-earth and focused on her work. She expects her pioneering mRNA research to be used in treatments for heart disease, cancer, diabetes, and many other ailments. As far as she, Weissman, and many other scientists are concerned, the COVID vaccine is only the beginning.

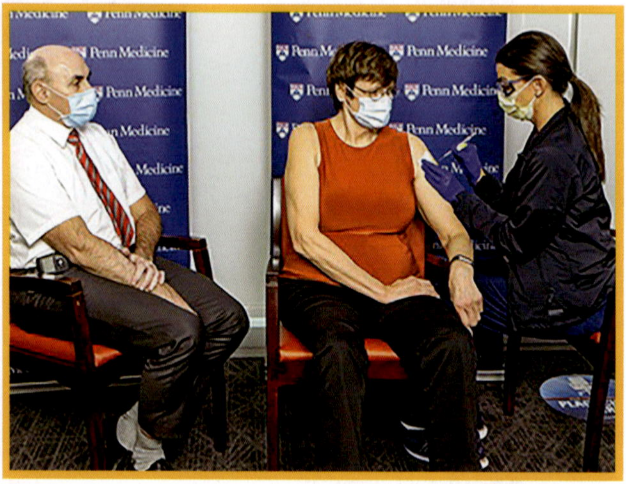

Karikó (*middle*) receives the Pfizer-BioNTech COVID vaccine with colleague Drew Weissman (*left*).

CHAPTER

1

AMBITIOUS YOUNG GIRL

Young Kati Karikó had never met a scientist, but she always wanted to be one. Nothing excited her more than learning new things and investigating the world around her, especially plants and animals. What made flowers grow? Why did animals act the way they did? She never tired of asking such questions.

Born on January 17, 1955, Kati grew up in the town of Kisújszállás on the Great Hungarian Plain, a large natural grassland in Europe. Surrounded by abundant vegetation and wildlife as well as vast herds of cattle, it was a wonderful place for a girl with her interests to live.

But the town had yet to catch up with the rest of the world in modern technology. Kati lived with her parents, Janos and Zsuzsanna Karikó, and older sister, also Zsuzsanna, in a small adobe house with a thatched reed roof. The family had no running water, refrigerator, or television. Kati didn't miss these conveniences because none of her friends had them either. The only heat in the long, cold winters came from a sawdust stove. Her family kept chickens and pigs for eggs and meat. When they needed milk, they went to their next-door neighbors, who had a cow.

Kati's father was a butcher, and her mother was a bookkeeper. Although they lacked much formal education, they had sharp, quick minds and stood up for their beliefs. Because Hungary was controlled by the Union of Soviet Socialist Republics (USSR), a former country in eastern Europe and Asia that existed from 1922

In 1920 World War I officially ended with the signing of the Treaty of Trianon. This treaty redistributed around two-thirds of Hungarian land to surrounding countries. Hungary had been part of Austria-Hungary, one of the Central or Axis powers, until Austria-Hungary's collapse during the war in 1918.

Two-year-old Kati Karikó (*second from left*) is pictured here with her parents and older sister in 1957.

to 1991, this could be a dangerous thing to do. Freedom of speech and political opposition were not tolerated by the Soviet regime and could lead to serious repercussions. As a one-year-old, Kati was too young to understand the Hungarian Revolution of 1956, but she almost certainly grew up hearing stories of the angry protests calling for Hungary's political freedom and an end to Soviet rule. Fierce fighting broke out in the streets of Budapest as Soviet tanks arrived to quell the rebellion, which persisted for days. Twenty-five hundred people died, and over the next several months more than two hundred thousand people left the country as refugees. Kati's father was arrested, along with many others, for supporting the rebellion and condemning the occupying government's oppressive policies. He was found guilty and given a suspended sentence, so he didn't serve time in prison, but he was fired from his job.

"When You Have Nothing"

Unable to obtain a full-time job, Janos was forced to take odd jobs. In the spring he sheared sheep, and in the summer he did

While the Hungarian Revolution lasted only several weeks, it expressed the Hungarians' desire for national independence from the Soviet regime. Similar uprisings occurred in other USSR states, including Georgia, Moldova, Lithuania, and more.

construction or temporary farmwork. Sometimes Kati and her sister joined him in the fields, doing simple tasks such as turning over cantaloupes so that each side got the benefit of the sun and the fruit grew evenly. In the winter he privately butchered pigs for families. "You learn so much from hardship," Kati recalls these difficult times. "You gain strength, stamina, and strong will. When you have nothing you are brave and honest as you have nothing to lose."

Thanks to her father's resolve to continue working as a butcher, Kati was exposed from an early age to animal anatomy. When she was about five, she watched her father cut up the carcass of a pig he had slaughtered for the market. The way the pig's bones and muscles fit together fascinated her. Witnessing the birth of a calf proved to be another memorable experience. Young as she was, Kati wanted to know more.

Despite living under Soviet rule, Kati's family was happy. Their modest home was filled with music, laughter, and love. They had everything they needed, plus a few extra luxuries, such as the violin her father loved to play and the girls' bicycle. Since bicycles weren't common in the neighborhood, Kati and Zsuzsanna shared theirs so that all their friends could learn to ride. When she wasn't pedaling down the roads, Kati enjoyed running, sports, and taking care of plants. Watching plants change as they grew piqued her curiosity. The plants in and around her home thrived under her attentive care.

Kati's hardworking parents wanted the best for their daughters. They stressed the importance of education and encouraged Kati and her sister to do well in school. In 1955, when Kati was ten, her father was finally able to get a permanent job. He purchased a hundred-year-old house in desperate need of restoration and then spent over two years carefully dismantling and rebuilding it. Kati and Zsuzsanna pitched in during the summers, cleaning mud and moss from the dilapidated structure. They helped remove bent nails and straighten them so that they could be used again. The family's arduous but enthusiastic efforts resulted in an attractive, habitable house with indoor plumbing and a separate bedroom for Kati and Zsuzsanna.

Enthusiastic Student

Whether helping restore a house or doing schoolwork, Kati pursued the job diligently. She excelled as a student. Her teachers appreciated her energy, curiosity, and desire to learn everything that she could. In eighth grade, she qualified for a national biology competition held in the capital city of Budapest. Foregoing a planned family trip to a water park, fourteen-year-old Kati was on her own as she traveled about 95 miles (153 km) by train from her hometown to the dormitory where she would stay. During the five-day competition, organizers tested many branches of biological knowledge. The students labeled plants that they gathered in nearby fields and assorted bones. Questions about animals and human anatomy also made up an important part of the competition. Although she was one of the youngest participants, Kati placed third and won a Russian-made camera, which she enjoyed for many years.

Kati's strong interest in the eighteenth-century Swedish physician and botanist Carl Linnaeus may have helped her place so well in the competition. In eighth grade she wrote a paper on Linnaeus and the system he invented for classifying plants and animals. In Linnaeus's system, each organism was divided into genus and species. Kati shared his fascination with categorizing living things.

Kati's biology teacher, Albert Tóth, was delighted with her accomplishments and encouraged her to pursue her ambitions. Besides enjoying his class at her school, she participated in his summer camp to study Hortobágy, a large region of prairies and wetlands in the Great Hungarian Plain. At the camp, she learned

In 1968 Kati (*front row, third from right*) attended Tóth's summer camp. One summer, when she was already enrolled in a university, she even helped Tóth lead a camp, encouraging students in their studies of plants and animals.

about her cultural heritage and the ecology of the Hungarian countryside that she called home.

Kati continued to enjoy the help and support of her teachers throughout high school. At sixteen, she had already decided on a career in biology and set her sights on the top-rated University of Szeged, some 90 miles (145 km) south of Kisújszállás. She would be competing with students from all over Hungary for a spot at the university, but her school was not highly rated academically. Even though she was a top student, her grades wouldn't impress the university. Many applicants would be better qualified than she was. Her English was limited, and a lot of the scientific papers she would have to read for her studies were in English. She lacked many advantages, such as enriching travel or educational experiences,

A Teacher's Confidence

Karikó's elementary school biology teacher, Albert Tóth, kept in touch with her after she graduated. In the early 1990s, he visited her in the United States, where she shared her research with him. Although Tóth didn't understand everything she was doing, he had confidence in her abilities. Years later, when he learned that her experiments with mRNA had made the COVID-19 vaccines possible, he said he wasn't surprised. He always knew she would do something important.

that some other applicants may have had. Knowing she needed more guidance than her modest high school offered, she enrolled in two of the university's preparatory camps for students from disadvantaged high schools. With her usual enthusiasm, she immersed herself in the camp's classes and activities.

Something else inspired Kati too—music. Whenever she felt especially challenged, she turned to her favorite song, "Diamonds and Gold," by popular Hungarian musician Zorán Sztevanovity. The lyrics celebrate the value of earning your own reward. Diamonds and gold, says the song, shine brighter when you dig them out of the earth yourself than when someone hands them to you. Nothing had ever been handed to her, but Kati never minded hard work. She welcomed it.

Waiting to hear from the university admissions office must have been an anxious time. Kati had done everything she could to beat the odds, but so had many other students. Only a small number could be admitted. Would she be among them?

At last, the anticipated letter arrived. Years of study and hard work had paid off. The whole family could relax and celebrate Kati's acceptance.

Hans Selye

Hans Selye was a Hungarian Canadian doctor, famous for his research on the way stress impacts health. Kati read his book, *The Stress of Life*, when she was sixteen. His idea that too much stress can harm the human body and that people should not worry about matters out of their control made a great deal of sense to her. As a school assignment, Kati and her classmates composed a letter to Selye. They didn't expect an answer, but they were thrilled when one arrived. The interest Selye took in the young people of a small remote town made Kati feel special. She and her classmates felt empowered to achieve their goals as scientists, doctors, teachers, or whatever else they wanted to be. Many years later, she still recalls how deeply she appreciated Selye's response. It is a legacy she seeks to pass on to others by trying to answer the letters she receives. "I also once received a letter in a small town," she explains.

Hans Selye, director of the University of Montreal's Institute of Experimental Medicine and Surgery, in 1950

When they were married in 1980, Béla Francia (*left*) was twenty years old and Karikó (*right*) was twenty-five.

College Life

Karikó began her first year at the University of Szeged in 1973. She was one of only twenty students (ten women and ten men) accepted into the biology program that year. Classes and labs kept her busy from early morning till late at night. But she found her courses on topics such as genetics, organic chemistry, and microbiology interesting and challenging, and she worked hard to excel in all these subjects. She did so well in her studies that she received the People's Republic Study Scholarship three years in a row. The money from this high honor enabled her to focus on her studies without worrying about finances.

The university's urban campus with its stately buildings couldn't have been more different from her quiet hometown. But Karikó found the bustling environment invigorating. She lived in a large dormitory where she made many friends and participated in a variety of social activities. She enjoyed going to discos and dancing to pop music. During her senior year, in 1977, she met a smart, friendly engineering student, Béla Francia, at an annual celebration sponsored by the biology department. The two discovered they had many interests in common and began to see a great deal of each other. After dating for three years, they decided to get married.

By then, Karikó had graduated with a bachelor's degree in biology. Since Szeged was the top-rated university in Hungary, she decided to stay to earn her PhD. Later, she would remember her time at Szeged as "the happiest years of my life."

CHAPTER 2

ONE-WAY TICKET

Karikó's life seemed to be working out just the way she always hoped it would. In addition to her studies at the university, she continued her undergraduate job as a research assistant at the prominent Biological Research Centre in Szeged, part of the Hungarian Academy of Sciences. Under the mentorship of the accomplished biochemists there, Karikó deepened her commitment to explore the chemical processes and substances that sustain life. She thrived in the stimulating environment of the lab.

Threatened by the Secret Police

Then, one night in 1978, the Hungarian secret police appeared at her door. The Soviet regime wanted to recruit her for its counterespionage efforts. By enlisting scientists as secret agents, the government had developed a network of researchers to report on colleagues who tried to smuggle significant findings out of the country. Even though twenty-two years had passed, as the daughter of a man found guilty of criticizing the Soviet

Karikó working at the Biological Research Centre in Szeged.

government, Karikó could be forced out of her profession if she refused. Her family might also face repercussions.

The idea of spying on her fellow researchers or getting anyone into trouble horrified her but so did the idea of her family being threatened because of her actions. Many years later, Karikó explained her predicament. "I knew how the system worked. I was afraid, so I signed the recruitment document," she admits. But her signature was just that—a signature. "I did not give any written report, I did not harm anyone," she declared.

The Molecule of Life

What Karikó did do was work hard and learn everything that she could about the structure and inner workings of living cells. It was an exciting time to be a biologist. Scientists were learning more and more about deoxyribonucleic acid (DNA), the complex substance found in the nucleus of every living cell. Sometimes called the molecule of life, DNA directs the development, survival, and reproduction of all living creatures by instructing cells to make the proteins that are vital to the cell's continued well-being. Proteins direct all the body's activities such as metabolism, digestion, growth, and healing from an injury.

DNA has four different chemical building blocks, or nucleotides. A single piece of double-stranded DNA may contain thousands of these four nucleotides in any one of millions of orders. The positioning or sequencing of these nucleotides tells the cell which protein to make.

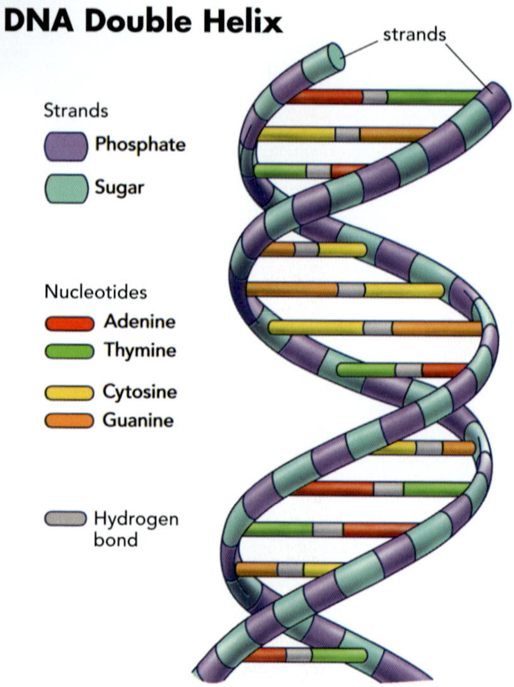

Nucleotides bind together in pairs using hydrogen bonds to hold together the two strands of DNA. These combinations, called base pairs, only occur between certain nucleotides. Adenine only binds to thymine, and cytosine only binds to guanine.

Sequencing DNA

By the late 1970s, when Karikó was beginning her career, scientists were making revolutionary progress in the way they sequenced DNA. Researchers developed techniques that allowed them to sequence hundreds of nucleotides at once. Although this number is small compared to the billions of nucleotides in DNA, it represented a tremendous breakthrough. Scientists could sequence simple viruses and better understand how these organisms infect living cells.

Fred Sanger was a genetic researcher who pioneered a method of sequencing DNA called Sanger sequencing. The technique involves chemical and electrical processes to determine the order of nucleotides in a DNA sample. In the final readout, the dark lines indicate the presence of a nucleotide.

But one question continued to puzzle researchers. How did the instructions to make a protein go from the DNA, which was bundled up in the cell's nucleus, to the rest of the cell, where the protein would actually be made? Scientists answered this in the 1950s with the discovery of a molecule that would later be called messenger RNA (mRNA). The code sequence to make a particular protein is copied from DNA into mRNA, which transports it out of the nucleus and into the cytoplasm, a jellylike substance of water, salt, and organic molecules that surrounds the nucleus. There, tiny structures, or ribosomes, receive the mRNA and follow the coded instructions to make proteins by linking amino acids together in the order specified by the mRNA, a process called translation. When the ribosomes are done translating the mRNA, enzymes break it down into smaller molecules to be used to create new mRNA.

As a graduate student just beginning work at the research center, Karikó knew little about mRNA. Her first assignment was to the lipid department, a specialty many biologists considered boring. But Karikó enjoyed learning a technique to wrap blood plasma and DNA in a lipid (fatty) coating and deliver it into cells. The ultimate goal would be to cure genetic diseases by incorporating corrective DNA into the DNA that already existed in the cells.

As Karikó was working in the lab one day in 1978, the head of the RNA research team dropped in. Perhaps a conversation with Karikó's supervisor, who valued her dedication and hard work, influenced what happened later: Karikó was assigned a place on the RNA team. "So everything was by chance," she told an interviewer in 2022. "I did not come up with the idea to work with RNA but of course, when I started to work there, I found it very exciting." Although she had no chance to work with mRNA, she was aware of its discovery and thought it might make a significant difference in curing disease. If the instructions that mRNA carried could be manipulated, researchers could control the proteins the cell made.

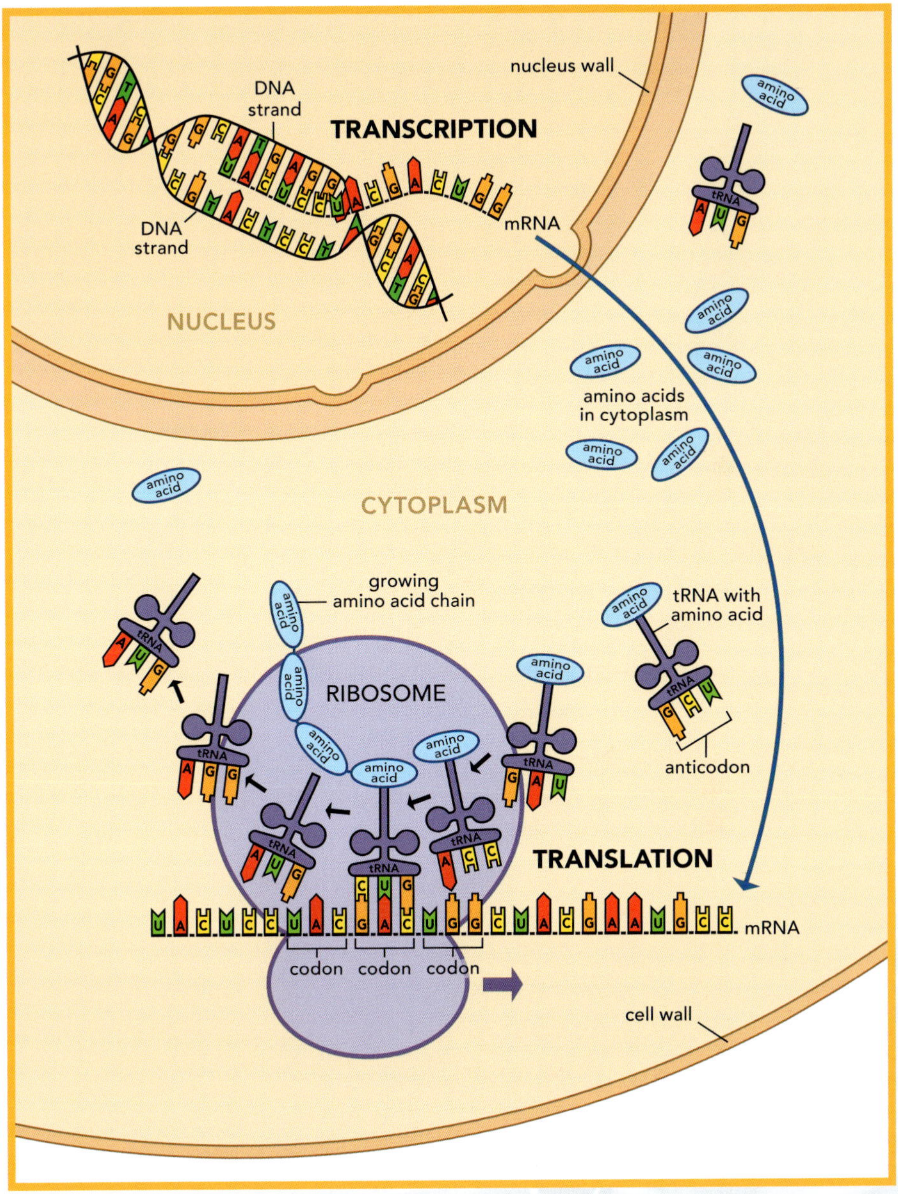

The mRNA code for a protein is made up of multiple codons—sequences of three nucleotides that each code for a specific amino acid. Anticodons on transfer RNA (tRNA) correspond with mRNA's codons and indicate which amino acid the tRNA should add to the chain.

The Discovery of mRNA

In 1956 two scientists at the Oak Ridge National Laboratory in Oak Ridge, Tennessee, Elliot "Ken" Volkin and Lazarus Astrachan, conducted an important experiment. They infected cells of the bacterium *Escherichia coli* (*E. coli*) with a virus. The scientists found that the virus turned off the bacteria's mechanism for making proteins and substituted its own instructions. It did this by making a single-stranded molecule that copied the virus's own double-stranded DNA. Following the new instructions from this molecule, the bacteria would make the virus's proteins instead of its own proteins. Volkin and Astrachan determined that the new short-lived molecule transported the instructions from the nucleus into the cytoplasm. The two scientists published their work, detailing the discovery of this new molecule, a nucleic acid, in the *Journal of Virology* in 1956. They continued to publish papers through 1958 describing their discovery, which they called "DNA-like RNA."

Volkin and Astrachan's findings differed from the accepted theories. Volkin believed this was why their work did not receive more attention. But the scientific establishment started to come around when other biologists began experimenting in 1957 and made the same discovery. In 1959 Arthur Pardee, François Jacob, and Jacques Monod, working in the Pasteur Institute in France, published the results of what was later called the PaJaMo experiment (the first two letters of each researcher's surname). They were studying how the gene for metabolizing the sugar lactose was turned on and off in bacteria. Meanwhile, Francis Crick and Sydney Brenner at

In 1962 Francis Crick (*shown*) and his colleagues James Watson and Maurice Wilkins were awarded the Nobel Prize in Physiology or Medicine for their discoveries of the structure of DNA and how it transfers information. Rosalind Franklin, who captured the image of DNA that Crick and Watson studied, was not credited.

Cambridge University in England were investigating how information coded in bacterial DNA directed protein synthesis. In April 1960 members of both groups attended a conference at Cambridge where Crick and Brenner suddenly realized that all these scientific findings could be explained by a messenger molecule, later named mRNA by Jacob and Monod. New experiments planned after that meeting confirmed the existence of mRNA.

"I have no hard feelings," Volkin later remarked about not receiving credit for the discovery. "That's the way things were." He died in 2011. His daughter Karen Lee Brunner thought of her father as she received her first COVID vaccine. Proudly, she told the nurse of her father's role in codiscovering mRNA.

"This Is the Way I Learned Science"

The Biological Research Centre in Szeged was sometimes short of essential laboratory resources because reagents manufactured in the Western countries were embargoed, or officially banned. So "it was more challenging to [conduct experiments] behind the Iron Curtain," explained Karikó, referring to the political division dividing Communist countries such as the Soviet Union and Hungary from the rest of the world. When she and her colleagues needed special bubbles of fat (liposomes) to enclose genetic material for their experiments, they could not order them from a biological supply company. Instead, they had to isolate their own phospholipids out of cow brains from the local slaughterhouse. They used the phospholipids to create the necessary liposomes. In 2020 Karikó shared the experience with the *Washington Post*. "This is the way I learned science," she explained, "always, that there is no problem. You cannot buy something? You make it."

Those proteins would affect the activities and health of the cell, maybe even cure disease. The potential for new medical treatments was enormous. Meanwhile, Karikó was able to isolate ribosomal RNA (rRNA), the type of RNA that forms part of the ribosomes where proteins are assembled.

A Clever Plan

After receiving her PhD in 1982, Karikó continued to work at the research center. That same year, she gave birth to a baby girl, whom she and Francia named Zsuzsanna (who goes by Susan). Watching their child grow, doing scientific research, and enjoying many close friendships, Karikó and her husband were settling into their lives as professional scientists and parents.

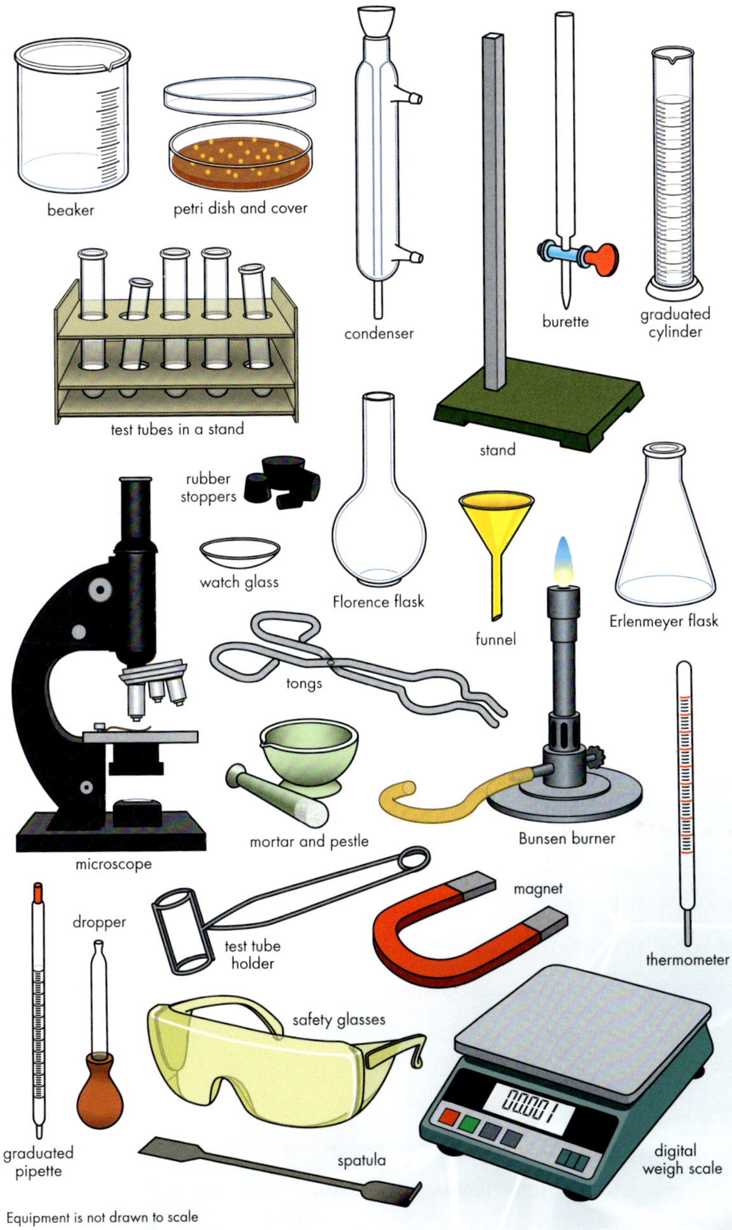

These common scientific instruments are some of the equipment Karikó and her colleagues used in their labs.

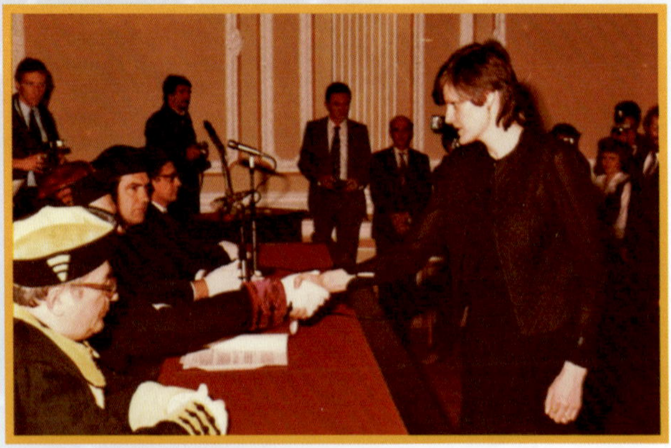

Karikó receives her PhD diploma from the University of Szeged.

Karikó's thirtieth birthday, in 1985, should have been a day of celebration, but it brought unwelcome news when she learned that the Biological Research Centre had lost government funding and she would soon be without a job. Suddenly, her secure future was replaced with uncertainty. Where could she find another job? How would the change affect her family?

A thorough job search in Hungary didn't turn up positions that allowed her to pursue science vigorously, designing experiments and solving problems. "I can do better than this," she said of the disappointing job offers she received. With Francia's full support, she made the difficult decision to seek a position in a foreign country. At first, Karikó tried to find a job elsewhere in Europe. When that search proved unsuccessful, she turned to the United States. After several months, she was offered a low-level position at Temple University in Philadelphia, Pennsylvania. The thought of moving so far away, adapting to a whole new culture, and leaving her parents, sister, and friends overwhelmed Karikó. She didn't know anyone in the United States, and she realized she would never return to live in Hungary permanently. "It was going to be a one-way trip," she later recalled.

Karikó wasn't the only Hungarian who felt compelled to exit the country. To discourage citizens from leaving, the government

Zsuzsanna holds onto her teddy bear, the very same toy in which her parents would later illegally hide extra cash as they immigrated to the United States.

severely limited the amount of money that could be taken out of the country. Karikó and Francia knew they could never get by on $100, the sum of their allotment. How would they buy groceries or pay the rent before Karikó received her first paycheck? Then they thought of a clever plan. They sold their car on the black market for an amount equal to $1,200 (about $3,300 currently). For their trans-Atlantic flight, Karikó sewed this illegal amount of money into Zsuzsanna's teddy bear. Unaware of her pivotal role, the two-and-a-half-year-old clutched her cherished toy tightly as the family headed toward the airport. None of the customs officials at the airport thought to examine a teddy bear, and the family boarded their flight without incident.

CHAPTER 3

THROWN INTO THE DEEP WATER

Karikó's plane touched down at JFK airport in New York City on July 31, 1985, in the aftermath of a fierce storm that had caused many flights to be canceled. Fighting jet lag, making their way through jams of people, Karikó, Francia, and Zsuzsanna made their connecting flight, arriving very late in Philadelphia. A representative from Temple University, recognizable for his unusually tall height, met them and drove them to temporary accommodations. En route, Karikó watched the lights outlining the historic boathouses along the Schuylkill River, a spectacular first view of the United States.

The next day brought overwhelming challenges. Karikó remembered her and her family's first days in the country as a time of confusion and stress. "When you leave a country without money and acquaintances, you will need all your knowledge and you will have to fight hard to stand your ground," she recalled in 2021. She compared her early days in America to being thrown into deep water. "The powers within you that you don't even know about come to the surface," she said. Struggling to keep afloat, Karikó and Francia had to find a place to live, learn a new currency, buy food, and arrange for transportation. They had no credit cards, no phone, and an incomplete mastery of English. On top of the still-pending, urgent household tasks, Karikó had to begin her new position at the university the day after their arrival in Philadelphia.

"A Shoestring Budget"

Working in the biochemistry department under a senior scientist, Karikó investigated an experimental RNA treatment for acquired immunodeficiency syndrome (AIDS), which lowers the body's ability to fight infection and disease. But although the work fascinated her, other aspects of the job proved discouraging. Her boss was hard to get along with, and her salary of $17,000 (about $47,000 in 2022) was scarcely enough for a family of three.

Unable to find a job as an engineer, Francia became the manager of a nearby apartment complex. Although he made the same amount of money as Karikó, they still had to budget carefully, never spending more than $30 (about $83 in 2022) a week for food. "I know how to have a shoestring budget," she recalled of this challenging time. Since their apartment didn't have a washing machine, Karikó had to haul all their dirty clothes to the basement of a neighboring building to get the laundry done. But although life was tough, Karikó and Francia remained optimistic about their American adventure. In the evenings, Karikó enjoyed cooking for her family. Traditional Hungarian dishes gave them a taste of home, and she occasionally tried Italian recipes. Six months after their arrival in the United States, Karikó's mother came for an extended visit and to help with childcare. The entire family enjoyed the fresh bread she baked because she didn't like American store-bought bread.

Scientific journals contain articles explaining the experiments and research that scientists have completed. Articles go through a rigorous review process before being published to make sure they are accurate. The most impactful research is published in prestigious, well-known journals such as *Nature*.

After several years at Temple University, Karikó found a better-paying job at Johns Hopkins University in Maryland. But her good fortune didn't last long. Angry at the prospect of losing a smart, hardworking researcher, her boss at Temple University tried to have her deported. Karikó not only lost the new position, but she and her husband were forced to go to court to defend their right to remain in the United States.

Once their legal status was resolved, Karikó took a position at the naval hospital in Bethesda, Maryland, even though it meant a commute of almost 139 miles (224 km). Because of the distance, Karikó spent most of her time on the job, returning home only for weekends.

In Bethesda, Karikó's workday started at 6 a.m. when she set up her experiments. Then she often made time for a run around the hospital campus. After putting in long hours at the lab, she spent her evenings in the library reading scientific papers. Bedtime meant staying at a friend's apartment or rolling out a sleeping bag in the lab. On weekends, she took equipment that was not functioning correctly back to Philadelphia for her husband to repair.

"We Felt Like We Could Do Anything"

At the naval hospital, Karikó learned a great deal about molecular biology, macromolecules (extremely large molecules such as DNA), and nucleotides, the basic building blocks of DNA. But she missed evenings with her family, and the commute was grueling. In the summer of 1989, Karikó accepted a position as an adjunct professor at the University of Pennsylvania. Delighted to be living at home again as Zsuzsanna progressed to second grade, Karikó

Karikó pauses while working at one of the labs at the University of Pennsylvania.

approached her new job with enthusiasm and energy. "You are not going to work—you are going to have fun," Francia often teased her as she left for the university in the early morning hours.

Karikó couldn't deny the joy she took in her work. Her salary was still modest, and she didn't have her own lab. But new developments in the field had made her research more exciting than ever. By 1989 scientists had discovered a way to synthesize mRNA in the lab. The major breakthrough made all kinds of experiments possible. "For scientists working on mRNA, this was very empowering," Karikó told the publication *Wired* in 2020. "Suddenly we felt like we could do anything."

A medical ward lay across the hallway from the lab where Karikó worked, and she could see patients through its window. Their presence moved and inspired her. "We have to take it (our science) to the patients," Karikó told her colleague as she gestured to the window. "We have to take it there." More than anything, she wanted to contribute to the treatment and cure of diseases. What happened in the lab had to make a difference.

Promising Results

Karikó could hardly wait to get started. Working in the lab of Dr. Elliot Barnathan, her research partner, she hoped to show that cells in culture (cells grown in a lab) would take up synthetic mRNA and make a complicated protein as instructed by the lab-created mRNA, one that the cells would not otherwise have produced. She and Barnathan used radioactive amino acids to determine if their experiment worked. The amino acids would attach to the newly created protein if it was produced. After they flushed out the proteins normally found in the cells as well as any unattached amino acids, they placed the residue in vials and ran them through a gamma counter, an instrument that detects radiation emitted by unstable atoms as they disintegrate. If the gamma counter detected radiation, that would indicate the presence of a protein that the synthetic mRNA had directed the cells to make.

Although most of their colleagues dismissed the idea as impractical—perhaps even foolish—the researchers had high hopes for their experiment. Anxiously, they waited by the dot matrix printer that was attached to the gamma counter. With mounting excitement, Karikó and Barnathan watched the printout emerge from the printer. The results were just what they had hoped for. The gamma counter detected the radiation that indicated the presence of the desired protein.

Countless possibilities suddenly loomed before them. Could mRNA help patients facing heart surgery? Could it make human cells live longer? Karikó felt that, in time, their work would have a major impact on treating many diseases.

Expected to Quit

Despite their success, Barnathan decided to leave the university and join a biotechnology firm. Again, Karikó found herself in a serious dilemma. She had no funding to support her experiments and no lab of her own. To remain at the university, she would have to partner with another senior scientist. "They [university officials] expected I would quit," Karikó remembered years later.

Dr. David Langer, a neurosurgeon who knew Karikó from his days as a medical student in Barnathan's lab, disagreed with the university officials. He was impressed with Karikó's dedication, and he believed in the potential of mRNA to treat illness. He had been attempting to use mRNA to make proteins that would cause blood vessels to dilate, or enlarge, thereby alleviating the danger of blood clots to patients who had suffered strokes. On Langer's recommendation, the chair of neurosurgery accepted Karikó into the department. This allowed Karikó to work with Langer on his mRNA projects.

Home Life

As usual, Karikó rose before daylight, leaving for work before her daughter was out of bed. She and Francia coordinated their schedules carefully so one of them would always be available to take Zsuzsanna to school and pick her up in the afternoon. Because of their wildly different work schedules, they sometimes used their child to communicate with each other. After school, Karikó might ask Zsuzsanna what her father had said earlier in the day. In turn, while Karikó was at work, her daughter would pass on any messages from her mother. During spring breaks, Karikó took Zsuzsanna to work with her.

Although daily life was sometimes challenging, Karikó found ways to make it happy. Trips to Hungary gave Zsuzsanna the chance to know her relatives and learn about her homeland. In Philadelphia, Francia had decided to remodel their home and spent hours crafting furniture. The whole family was proud of his creations. Karikó continued to cook Hungarian dishes and took to baking chocolate cakes from scratch. At night she snacked on peanut M&Ms. Hearing the rattle of the candy falling into the dish, Zsuzsanna would hurry over to share the treat.

Karikó's enthusiasm for work spilled over into evenings with her family. On one evening in 1993, she summoned Francia and eleven-year-old Zsuzsanna into her study. "You have to sit down and now listen to my argument!" she said. She proceeded to explain that mRNA broke down very quickly in cells. She thought she had found a way to make it last longer. This meant that it would have more time to instruct cells to make proteins that could help fight diseases.

Her husband and daughter listened carefully. "Oh, my gosh, fantastic!" they exclaimed. Even though they couldn't grasp all that she was telling them, they shared her excitement and knew her work was important.

mRNA Hustler

When things didn't go well, Karikó shared her discouragements too. An idea that seemed promising one day might turn out to be a dead end. The hopeful vision she'd shared with Francia and Zsuzsanna didn't lead to the results she anticipated. Her attempts with Langer to use mRNA to dilate blood vessels also proved disappointing. Their experiments would not lead to a way to help stroke patients after all. Most people might have considered their efforts a failure. Karikó viewed their results in a much more positive light. "It seems that the experiment didn't work," she told *Glamour* magazine in 2021. But the experiment had succeeded in showing her what wouldn't work. Her assumptions had been inaccurate, and she could always trust science to get her on the right track.

Sometimes she turned to Renaissance-era artist, scientist, and engineer Leonardo da Vinci to make her point. "Experiments never err, your expectations do," da Vinci had said. Karikó enjoyed paraphrasing his words.

Karikó continued to read scientific papers and to attend professional conferences where scientists gathered to share recent results and network with one another. She also wrote grant applications for funding to support her research. Since universities and private labs cannot always afford to provide all the funding scientists need to carry on their work, researchers turn to organizations such as the National Institutes of Health (NIH) and the National Science Foundation for financial support. As an mRNA scientist, Karikó needed money for chemicals, tissue cultures, growth medium and support for cells, specialized equipment, salaries for assistants, and much more. In completing a grant submission, applicants must thoroughly describe their research, what they hope to discover, and the methods and research they plan to use. They must explain the significance of their work,

"In the Shadow of Gene Therapy"

While Karikó was pushing mRNA's potential to cure and prevent diseases in the 1980s and 1990s, other scientists tended to be more interested in exploring the prospect of gene editing. The start of the Human Genome Project in 1990, which sought to identify the complete set of human genes and to make them available for research, stimulated a great deal of enthusiasm for curing diseases through genetic manipulation. As a result of this work, researchers developed a revolutionary technique called gene therapy.

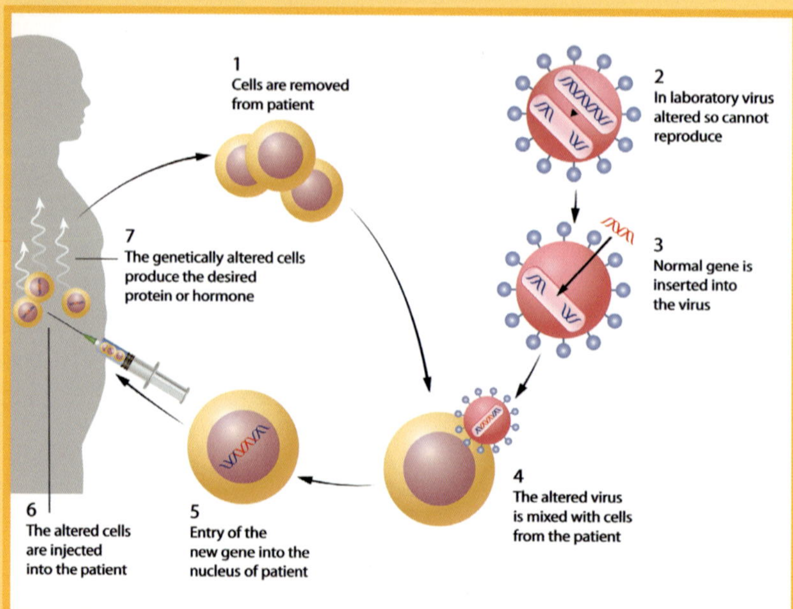

This diagram illustrates how gene therapy works. Doctors target a disease-causing gene in a patient's DNA, using a virus as a vector, or a carrier, to replace the disease-causing gene with a healthy version.

There are two types of gene therapy: gene editing (correcting a faulty gene) and gene addition (inserting a new healthy gene). And gene therapy can be administered in two ways. In ex vivo therapy, cells are removed from the body, corrected or replaced, and put back into the body. In vivo therapy involves making genetic corrections or replacing genes in cells that remain inside the body. This is achieved with a vector, or a virus, which transmits the new genes or the corrections.

Sickle cell anemia is one of the few diseases for which gene therapy exists. In the procedure, bone marrow cells are removed from the body, and the correct gene is inserted into those cells, which are returned to the patient. Acute lymphoblastic leukemia is another disease for which a gene therapy has been developed. Scientists hope to develop gene therapy for other illnesses such as metabolic disorders. "I was working in the shadow of gene therapy and people who work with DNA," Karikó said in 2021.

Unlike gene therapy, synthetic mRNA does not alter an organism's DNA. It instructs cells to make a protein to fight a specific illness or to induce immunity to a disease. Short-lived, the mRNA is cleared from the body after performing its function. Karikó believed this to be a more reasonable, and ultimately safer, approach than gene editing. "I always thought that the majority of patients don't need new genes," Karikó said in an interview with *Wired* magazine. "They need something temporary like a drug, to cure their aches and pains, so mRNA was always more interesting to me."

provide a history of its field, and submit biographies of all the researchers involved. A standard federal grant application may be fifteen to twenty-five pages, and competition is fierce. Statistics vary, but according to some sources only about 25 percent of applicants are funded.

When Karikó's applications were rejected, she kept on writing grants and attending conferences. She tried to convince the scientists she met of the potential of mRNA to treat illnesses. Her enthusiasm earned her the nickname "mRNA hustler." But despite her persistence, no one seemed interested in her arguments.

"I Work for Myself"

Karikó never stopped trying to convince people of the value of her research and to secure funding. One year she worked diligently on a grant proposal all through the holidays and New Year's Eve. "I'm sorry," she apologized to her sister, who was visiting from Hungary. "I need that money." The funding would make a critical difference in what she could accomplish in the lab. Once again she faced disappointment. Seven scientists from her university had submitted grant applications. Karikó's was the only one rejected.

No matter what she did, everything seemed stacked against Karikó. When she spoke at conferences, scientists sometimes asked the name of her supervisor, implying that someone else—not Karikó—had been behind her research, findings, and presentations. She attributed their error to a bias against women, especially those who spoke with an accent. No one considered her ideas with the seriousness they deserved.

Karikó's situation deteriorated when Langer decided to leave the University of Pennsylvania. She had no funding and no lab where she could test her ideas. Then things got even worse. In 1995 an issue with Francia's visa caused him to be detained in Hungary for six months. While he was gone, Karikó was diagnosed with cancer and told that she would require surgery to remove the tumor. Before the operation, the university informed her of a change in her employment status. Due to her lack of publications in scientific journals and her failure to win grants, she was being demoted and would receive a cut in salary. Under the circumstances, she was expected to resign.

But Karikó's research was more important to her than her salary or her academic status. She also had her daughter's future to consider. Without the substantial discount the university offered to children of faculty members, she could not afford to send Zsuzsanna to college. After her surgery successfully removed the tumor, she thought things over and decided to stay to continue working despite these setbacks and difficult circumstances. The university moved her to a small, ill-equipped office near where they housed lab animals. When the neurosurgery department hired a new chair, Karikó asked for a return to her previous position. Not only was her request denied, but the new head told her she was not "faculty material." Karikó refused to allow such harsh treatment to discourage her. Day after day, she continued to read medical journals and conduct experiments.

Although she was willing to forego a large salary and knew she would likely never be placed on a tenure track (pathway to promotion and a permanent position), Karikó demanded respect for a commitment that went far beyond such considerations. Once, at a party, she overheard one scientist remark to another, "Kati works for me."

A rare anger flashed in Karikó's eyes. "I don't work for you!" she declared. "Do you think that Saturday, Sunday I am here for you? I am here for me. I am here to learn more and to understand."

For Karikó, knowledge itself and the hope of a discovery that would improve patient care mattered more than anything else. These made all her sacrifices worthwhile.

CHAPTER 4

BREAKTHROUGH

Laden with several medical journals, Karikó waited to use the copy machine. She liked to have her own copies of newly published scientific papers that were pertinent to her field. In those days before publications were posted online, she had to find the relevant periodicals in the library and make hard copies.

When another researcher joined the queue with his own stack of articles to copy, Karikó introduced herself and began to talk about her work. "I am an RNA scientist," Karikó recalled of their conversation. "I can make anything with mRNA." Unlike most of her fellow scientists, the researcher, Drew Weissman, listened with great interest. He was a research immunologist, a doctor who studies the way the immune system protects people from infection and disease. He said that he had recently come to the University of Pennsylvania from the lab of Anthony Fauci, noted researcher and then director of the National Institute of Allergy and Infectious Diseases at the NIH. Weissman was hoping to use DNA to make a vaccine against the human immunodeficiency virus (HIV), which attacks the body's immune system. Potentially life-threatening, HIV leaves a person vulnerable to disease and infection, and if untreated, a patient with HIV can develop AIDS. Karikó offered an interesting suggestion. She could provide mRNA to be used in the vaccine instead of DNA.

Even though most scientists still considered mRNA research a dead end, Weissman thought the approach was worth considering. "If you make it, I'll try it," he told Karikó. Whatever he might have known about Karikó's lack of a lab or a grant didn't bother him. Weissman welcomed Karikó into his own lab and began working with her to introduce mRNA into cell cultures.

The two lab partners were very different in personality. While Karikó was outgoing and chatty, Weissman tended to be reserved. He rarely smiled or made small talk. But in their open-mindedness, commitment to research, and careful attention to detail, Karikó and Weissman were perfectly matched. "I am the enthusiastic, noisy one, and he's the quiet, thinking one," Karikó told *FT Magazine* in 2021. "But we have different knowledge, and we educated each other." Even at home, both scientists worked many hours into the night, emailing each other long after midnight and getting immediate replies.

A Devastating Disappointment

Weissman had been working with a specialized component of the immune system known as dendritic cells. These cells exist in the parts of the body that come into contact with external substances—such as air and food—and include the skin as well as the linings of the nose, lungs, stomach, and intestines. Because of their positioning, dendritic cells are among the first to encounter an antigen (a foreign material such as bacteria, a virus, or a chemical) in the body. Dendritic cells deliver antigens to immune cells called lymphocytes (B and T cells) that mount a strong immune response. B cells produce antibodies that circulate in the blood, and T cells have receptors to attack antigens directly.

Drew Weissman: "We Didn't Give Up"

Even as a child, Drew Weissman was organized, meticulous, and fascinated by science. He was also a hard worker with a strong sense of responsibility. On sailing expeditions with his sister and cousins, Drew happily did all the work while his companions relaxed.

In 1981 Weissman graduated from Brandeis University in Waltham, Massachusetts. In the four years it had taken his classmates to earn undergraduate degrees, he earned both a bachelor's and master's degree in science. Ten years later, he began working in Anthony Fauci's lab. It was a demanding and stimulating place to work. Doctors from all over the world called the lab with questions on diagnosing particular diseases. In Fauci's lab, Weissman began his study of dendritic cells. He was certain these cells held the key to developing vaccines for an assortment of diseases. Some day he hoped to set up his own lab to work with dendritic cells.

This photo of Weissman and Karikó, taken in 2015, shows a glimpse of their differing personalities.

Drew Weissman (*third from right*) is pictured here with his research team in 2001. Karikó appears third from left.

Weissman's chance came in 1997 when he was recruited by the chair of infectious diseases at the University of Pennsylvania. Setting up his own lab, he was eager to conduct experiments with dendritic cells that might lead to a vaccine for HIV. Then he met Karikó, with whom he would face hardship, disappointment, and ultimately success. A scientist who joined Weissman's lab in 2005 recalled his mentor's method for solving knotty problems. When something puzzled Weissman in the lab, he would give himself a job to do at home. He might repair the plumbing, construct a deck, or even build an addition. Focusing on a physical task seemed to clear his mind and often helped him find the solution to his scientific problem.

On receiving an honorary degree from Drexel University's College of Medicine in 2021, Weissman reflected on his and Karikó's success. "The person who achieves his goal is the one that has faced frustration and dealt with it, understood it, and used it to their advantage," he told his audience of newly graduated doctors. "[Kati Karikó] and I repeatedly fell, were knocked down, ignored. And we kept getting up, and we didn't give up."

Enthusiastic Sports Mom

By the time Karikó met her colleague Drew Weissman, her daughter was in high school. Zsuzsanna, or Susan as she was known at school, was a talented and enthusiastic basketball player, an activity her mother encouraged. At her daughter's basketball games, Karikó yelled and gestured wildly, attracting so much attention that she embarrassed Susan. To prevent awkwardness, Susan asked her mother not to attend future games. Karikó left it to Francia to support Susan in a more restrained manner. But the proud parent that she was, she continued to take an eager interest in her daughter's athletic pursuits.

Karikó also provided an outstanding role model for Susan in her own physical endeavors. An enthusiastic runner since childhood, she had already run several half marathons when she decided to go for the complete experience—a full marathon of 26.2 miles (42.1 km). In preparation, she rose at 4 a.m. each morning to run about 6 to 12 miles (10 to 20 km). At the age of fifty, she completed the Philadelphia Marathon in four hours and thirty-one minutes.

How would mRNA affect this immune response? To help answer the question, Karikó provided mRNA for Weissman to add to cell culture dishes of B and T cells. But the cells did not produce the protein that the mRNA instructed them to make. Then Karikó and Weissman introduced mRNA into cultures with dendritic cells. This time, the dendritic cells created a vast amount of HIV Gag, the major structural protein of the HIV virus, which the scientists detected through an ingenious method. In addition to instructions for creating HIV protein in their synthetic mRNA, they had added directions for making luciferase, an enzyme that causes cells to produce light. If the cells in the culture dishes assembled HIV

CELLS OF THE IMMUNE SYSTEM

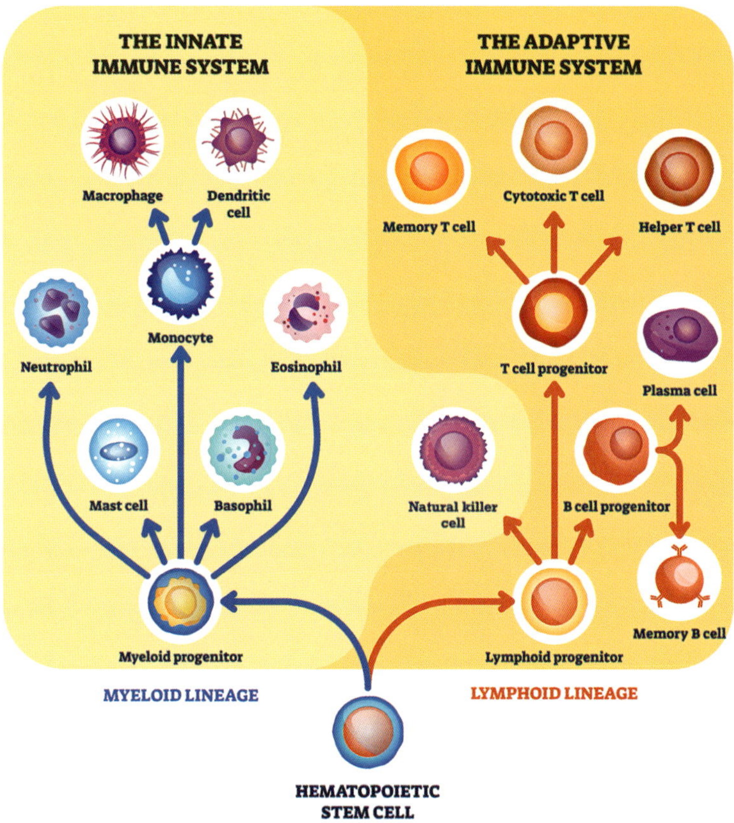

Stem cells are cells that have the potential to develop into one of many specific types of cell. The cells of the immune system form from stem cells. Dendritic cells, the kind that Drew Weissman studies, are one type of immune cell. T cells and B cells are some of the other kinds.

proteins, they would also make luciferase. Although the miniscule amount of light produced by single cells would be unnoticeable without a microscope, the cumulative effect of many cells lighting up would be more visible. Karikó and Weissman were thrilled when

Almost 95 percent of all laboratory animals are mice or rats. Mice are the most commonly used animal for biomedical research.

their culture dishes began to glow. This meant that a tremendous amount of HIV protein had been produced, exactly what they had hoped for.

The *Journal of Immunology* published the findings in 2000. Because of this significant accomplishment, Karikó and Weissman believed they were on a swift, straightforward path to develop a vaccine against the HIV virus. Their next step was to see what happened when they injected synthetic mRNA into a complete organism—an animal. Animal testing allows scientists to observe and evaluate the effect of an experimental procedure on the entire body instead of merely the cellular level. It is an important tool for assessing the safety and efficacy of a procedure. So Karikó and Weissman began experimenting with mice.

But something went seriously wrong. The mice became extremely ill after receiving the lab-created mRNA. Their bodies twisted, and their fur became ragged. They stopped running and eating. Some of them died. At first, Karikó and Weissman had no idea why.

Further investigations revealed that the mice's immune system was attacking the synthetic mRNA as a foreign substance. This provoked a severe inflammatory response with swelling and pain. Unless Karikó and Weissman could find a way to prevent this dangerous—potentially deadly—reaction, they would not be able to use mRNA to treat human ailments. "I had spent ten years trying to make a therapeutic protein-encoding mRNA, and all of it was useless," Karikó recalled years later.

A Vital Clue

But Karikó and Weissman refused to accept defeat. Instead, they focused their efforts on finding a way to prevent the body's immune system from attacking the synthetic mRNA. To start, they looked at the control group they had used in previous experiments. The control group was a set of mice that were not injected with the synthetic mRNA, receiving instead a different kind of RNA known as transfer RNA (tRNA). Not synthesized in a lab, this tRNA from cows and from bacteria could be purchased from chemical companies.

Karikó and Weissman noticed a big difference between the experimental group and the control group. The mice who got the natural tRNA, harvested from living cells, did not get sick the way the mice who received lab-made mRNA did. Here was a piece of information, a vital clue, that might just lead to a solution! Karikó thought about the four nucleotides that make up RNA. If the nucleotides in lab-made mRNA could be chemically adjusted to be more like tRNA, would this eliminate or reduce the immune response? Weissman agreed that it was worth trying.

Three Main Kinds of RNA

A number of kinds of RNA exist, but three main categories are used in protein synthesis.

- **Messenger RNA (mRNA) brings instructions for making a specific protein from the nucleus of a cell to the cytoplasm that surrounds it. mRNA comprises 5 percent of a cell's total RNA.**
- **Ribosomal RNA (rRNA) combines with enzymes and proteins found in the cytoplasm to create ribosomes. These complex structures provide support for translating the amino acids specified by mRNA into proteins.**
- **Transfer RNA (tRNA) brings the amino acids specified by the mRNA to the ribosomes.**

"Now We Can Use It"

Karikó and Weissman spent more than a year figuring out what changes in the nucleotides would prevent the body's immune system from targeting their synthetic mRNA as a foreign invader. Often arriving at the lab before sunrise and leaving late in the day, the research partners tried one version of mRNA after another. Eventually, their experiments led them to focus on the nucleotide named uridine. They noticed that sometimes uridine transformed naturally into a slightly different variant known as pseudouridine. When this happened, no dangerous inflammatory reaction occurred. Karikó and Weissman planned an experiment to test this information.

Concocting their own pseudouridine, they assembled yet another version of their synthetic mRNA and injected it into culture dishes of dendritic cells. After twenty hours, they harvested some of the cells to study with a flow cytometer, an instrument that allowed them to view cells clearly and individually. The presence of certain proteins on the surface of the cells would indicate that an immune response had been activated. The absence of the proteins would mean there was no immune response that could cause inflammation. After examining thousands of cells carefully, the researchers concluded that the lab-made mRNA had not generated an immune response. This finding was also supported by a careful testing of the supernatant, a fluid that scientists add to a cell culture to keep it alive. Karikó and Weissman tested samples of this fluid for protein markers of inflammation that the cells might have released. They found no such markers.

Karikó and Weissman were beside themselves with excitement. They had stopped the dendritic cells from targeting their lab-made mRNA as a foreign substance. This changed everything. "Oh my God," said Karikó. "Now we can use it." What their fellow scientists had rejected as a dead end suddenly seemed poised to revolutionize medicine.

CHAPTER 5

WHAT'S IT GOOD FOR?

Despite their stunning success, Karikó and Weissman's challenges were far from over. No one seemed interested in what they had accomplished with mRNA and pseudouridine. Their grant applications were rejected, and major medical journals declined to publish their findings. Karikó and Weissman knew they had discovered something tremendously important, but they needed support and financial backing to continue their work.

Things seemed to be looking up in 2005 when the scientific journal *Immunity* published their paper, "Suppression of RNA Recognition by Toll-Like Receptors: The Impact of Nucleoside Modification and the Evolutionary Origin of RNA." Surely, they thought, doctors and medical researchers would begin to recognize the vast potential of mRNA in healing diseases. "Our phones are going to ring off the hook," Weissman told Karikó. But days passed, then weeks. No one called to congratulate them

Karikó works in a lab at the University of Pennsylvania in 2005.

or ask questions. No one seemed to think they had accomplished anything significant. Their colleagues, publications, and the media continued to focus on gene therapy, especially with the completion of the thirteen-year-old Human Genome Project in 2003. This monumental accomplishment produced the sequencing of billions of nucleotides in human DNA. Thousands of researchers in the United States, France, Germany, Japan, China, and the United Kingdom took part in the effort. Their success made it possible to develop experimental gene therapies for certain metabolic disorders and generated a great deal of excitement, eclipsing interest in mRNA.

"This Is Unbelievable"

Lack of peer interest, though disappointing, did not dampen Karikó's and Weissman's enthusiasm for their work. Moving on from

The Human Genome Project ended in 2003, but the researchers had only sequenced about 92 percent of the human genome. They could not sequence the rest due to the limits of the technology they had at the time. The last 8 percent was finally completed in 2022.

cells to animal experiments, they injected their modified mRNA into mice. The mice showed no signs of inflammation and appeared perfectly healthy. Taking their experiments a step further, Karikó and Weissman programmed synthetic mRNA with instructions for making the protein erythropoietin (EPO). Then they injected the substance into monkeys. If all went as they hoped, the monkeys' cells would produce EPO that would stimulate the production of red blood cells.

The results proved successful beyond their imagining. Not only was there no inflammation, but the amount of EPO in the monkeys' blood increased drastically, leading to a rise in the number of red blood cells. For an instant, both scientists were speechless. "This is unbelievable," Weissman said at last. They hoped their significant finding would attract a good deal of scientific as well as corporate attention. Companies and researchers would surely race to develop and test mRNA treatments. Perhaps the long wait for recognition of their work was over at last.

"No One Would Listen"

But once again, Karikó and Weissman were baffled by the lack of interest in mRNA. Even officials at their own institution, the University of Pennsylvania, failed to understand the implications of their work. Hoping to patent their breakthrough, Karikó went to see the university's intellectual property officer. A patent, granted by the US patent office, would allow the university to keep control of their modified mRNA. But Karikó had to first convince the officer that their synthetic mRNA was worth patenting. As she explained, the man kept interrupting, "What's it good for?" Nothing Karikó said convinced him that her lab-made mRNA was worth his consideration.

Karikó was about to give up when she noticed the officer's bald spot. "You know what," she said, "mRNA would be good for growing hair."

"Really?" Suddenly, the man was fully engaged.

"Yes, it could be," said Karikó and launched an entirely new approach. This time, the officer listened attentively. At the end of her presentation, he agreed to apply for a patent.

It was a small victory, but broader recognition continued to elude Karikó and Weissman. What were they to do with their accomplishment? How could its potential be developed and made available to doctors and patients? Karikó and Weissman decided to launch their own company to develop drugs and treatments, but their efforts were fraught with difficulty. The University of Pennsylvania owned all procedures and discoveries made by researchers in its employ. To use their own synthetic mRNA, they

"We Wanted the Science Available to Everyone"

Karikó and Weissman were eager to share their knowledge and methods with other researchers. "We didn't want to patent the nucleotide-modified mRNA," Karikó told *Lifestyles Magazine*, "because we wanted everybody to use it. But we were told that if we didn't, nobody would develop it or invest in it. We wanted the science available to everybody—it wasn't about the money."

would have to be licensed by the university. But the university demanded a majority stake, giving it a controlling interest in the company and entitling it to half the proceeds that the company took in. Such an arrangement would make it extremely difficult for the founders to attract investors, who would also want a large portion of the profit. "They just asked for too much," Weissman explained.

Proud Mother

While Karikó and Weissman scrambled to get their company off the ground, exciting things were happening in Karikó's personal life. Her daughter had just graduated from the University of Pennsylvania. Susan Francia's love of athletics had grown to include many sports. At 6 feet 2 (1.9 m), she was a powerful rower, expert enough to strive for a place on the US Olympic team.

The competition for the team was tough. When she was exhausted or doubted herself, her mother encouraged her to stick to her goals. Karikó sang "Diamonds and Gold" to her daughter, the song emphasizing the rewards of hard work that had never ceased to inspire Karikó. It wasn't a new message. She had heard her mother sing the song many times before. But Karikó's support and example of determination and courage meant a great deal. All her life, Susan Francia had seen her mother fight the odds and never give up. She was not about to give up either. "She always said our work ethic was driving her," Karikó would say later.

The last two months before the announcement of the US roster were especially demanding, but Susan Francia's perseverance paid off with a place on the team. Karikó's reaction was joyful—and very vocal. "My mother was finally allowed to shout loudly (and now my father was embarrassed)," she would later recall humorously. "I couldn't ask for a better cheering section. Leading up to the Olympic final, I wanted more than anything to make my family proud."

In the summer of 2008, Susan Francia and her crewmates rowed to victory in Beijing, China. Full of joy and pride, Karikó and Béla

Karikó (*left*) celebrates the gold medal her daughter, Susan Francia (*middle*), won in the 2008 Beijing Olympics. Francia would go on to win another gold medal in the 2012 Olympics in London, England.

Going Backward

Karikó and her daughter see an interesting similarity between doing science experiments and rowing. Facing backward in the boat as they ply their oars, a rowing crew can't see how close they are to the finish line. As Karikó and Weissman strove to develop an mRNA technology that could be used to treat diseases, they didn't know how far they were from the finish line either. Comparing her mother's work with her own rowing, Susan Francia told ESPN that their goals "required a trust in the process that every pull, every step was getting us closer to the things we wanted to accomplish. Looking back now, it really did work out that way."

Susan Francia (*fourth from the front*) rows to victory with the US Olympic team in Beijing.

Francia watched their daughter receive her Olympic gold medal. Four years later, she and her rowing teammates captured the gold at the London Summer Olympics. Instead of being known as a biochemist, Karikó gained minor celebrity as the mother of an Olympic champion. The recognition amused and delighted her.

End of a Dream

Between the 2008 and 2012 Olympics, Karikó and Weissman's efforts to kick-start their own company ended. On February 5, 2010, they received a disappointing letter from the university. Since they had not been able to reach a licensing agreement concerning synthetic mRNA, the university wanted to license it to a third party. The company in question had no intention of using mRNA to develop new medical treatments. It manufactured reagents (chemical substances used in experiments), not drugs or other therapeutic agents.

This was not what Karikó wanted, but she and Weissman had no other options. They could not afford to license their own discovery. Karikó could scarcely keep from crying as she signed the letter agreeing to the deal. Her and Weissman's signatures meant that their company, RNARx, would not have access to their own technology. Although Karikó continued to do research at the University of Pennsylvania, the dream of running her own mRNA company was dead. She had been squeezed out by the university.

A Few People Take Note

While most of Karikó and Weissman's colleagues continued to ignore their work, a few people had read and grasped the importance of their groundbreaking paper and began to consider the potential of mRNA to treat disease. Uğur Şahin, a German doctor specializing in immunology and cancer treatments, and his physician wife, Özlem Türeci, were excited by the idea that mRNA might be used to make cancer vaccines. With funding from investors, they created a company to explore the possibilities. Taking sections of the words *biopharmaceutical*, *new*, and *technologies*, they named the company BioNTech.

Derrick Rossi, an assistant professor at Harvard Medical School, had also read Karikó and Weissman's paper with great interest. He believed that mRNA held the key to treating serious ailments such as spinal cord injuries and Parkinson's disease. Rossi founded a company to explore and develop the potential of mRNA therapies with Robert Langer, a biomedical engineering professor at the Massachusetts Institute of Technology; Noubar Afeyan, an entrepreneur responsible for dozens of biotech start-ups; and Harvard researcher Timothy Springer and cardiovascular scientist Kenneth Chien. Rossi combined words *modified* and *RNA* to name his company Moderna. In 2012, two years after the company's founding, Afeyan predicted that Moderna would be "adding an entirely new drug category to the pharmaceutical arsenal," a category based on lab-made mRNA.

Time for a Change

More than ever, Karikó wanted to see her method for assembling synthetic mRNA put to work in clinical settings. But the University of Pennsylvania still failed to recognize the significance of her work, and the NIH did not respond favorably to her grant applications. Despite her characteristic optimism, she couldn't help but feel let down.

During the summer of 2013, Karikó took time off to visit family and friends in Hungary. While there, she drove to Lucerne, Switzerland, to see her daughter compete in the third World Rowing Cup. En route back to Hungary, she stopped to visit BioNTech in Mainz, Germany, where she met with Şahin. The two eagerly shared their ideas on the future of mRNA research.

Uğur Şahin and Özlem Türeci, mRNA Pioneers

From their youngest years, Şahin and Türeci, the founders of BioNTech, were fascinated by science. The son of Turkish immigrants to Germany, Şahin devoured popular science books from the library. Türeci, whose family also came to Germany from Turkey, sometimes accompanied her father, a doctor, as he treated patients. When she was only six, she watched an operation to remove a patient's appendix and decided to learn all that she could about biology, with the intention of becoming a doctor.

Şahin and Türeci met as young doctors at a German hospital. With similar interests and strong work ethics, the two soon became a couple. In 2001 they founded Ganymed to develop drugs to treat cancer. They took the name from a Turkish phrase that means "earned through hard work." The saying fit their lives well. Even on their wedding day in 2002, they went straight from the ceremony back to the lab to work. They founded their second company, BioNTech, in 2008. As early as 2018, one year before the outbreak of COVID-19, Şahin predicted that mRNA could be used to create a vaccine if a worldwide pandemic broke out.

The founders of BioNTech, Uğur Şahin and Özlem Türeci, are immunologists. They consider it their purpose to help the immune system resist disease. Because of the success of the COVID-19 vaccine, their company is working on mRNA vaccines against malaria, certain forms of cancer, and other diseases.

Uğur Şahin and Katalin Karikó had just met each other in person for the first time when this photo was taken.

Karikó was delighted to find someone whose hopes and plans coincided so closely with her own. Equally impressed by Karikó's accomplishments and priorities, Şahin offered her a job that same day. "We need you," he said.

Karikó thought of all the hardships she had faced at the university, of the uphill battle to gain funding and to achieve the respect of most of her colleagues. In contrast, the researchers at BioNTech were excited about mRNA and interested in her ideas. Although it was still a relatively new company without any accepted medical therapies to its credit, Karikó felt certain it was on the right track. She struck a deal to join BioNTech.

Back in Philadelphia, Karikó made plans to move to Mainz. A resident of the United States for twenty-eight years, she had become a naturalized citizen in 1999, enjoying dual citizenship with Hungary. She loved her adopted country and valued the opportunities her immigration had made available to her. She would miss her lovely home and many friends. Since she couldn't know ahead of time how well she would adjust to the new environment, she and Francia, who supported her, decided not to pull up stakes completely. Her husband would remain in Philadelphia to stick with his job and to look after their house. If Karikó found life in Germany not to her liking, she could always return home.

Although Karikó hated to leave her family behind, she had no qualms about relinquishing her job at the university. Colleagues thought she was making a big mistake, and some made fun of her prospects. "BioNTech doesn't even have a website," they teased. But Karikó knew that she was taking an important step forward. Half playfully, half seriously, she told her supervisor not to change a thing in her lab. One day, she predicted, it would be a museum of her work.

CHAPTER

6

A TURNING POINT IN VACCINE SCIENCE

For the second time in her life, Karikó's mission to further science had led her to move halfway across the world. But this time, her husband and daughter had not come with her. "In my first week in Germany, I cried every night because I missed my family," she remembered. But she quickly settled into her position as senior vice president at BioNTech, a role she would have for many years. On first arriving at the company at the age of fifty-eight, Karikó did experiments with her own hands, developing her own way of doing things. Later, when she had a team, she decided to stay out of their way because she considered it important for them to figure out things for themselves and feared her constant instructions would make their work more difficult.

Karikó's life developed a new routine: she spent ten months of the year in Mainz and two months in Philadelphia. The family spent as much time together as they could, with Karikó welcoming periodic visits to Mainz from her husband and daughter. She felt that she had made the right decision in leaving academic research for the more immediate goals of a biotech company. "We [BioNTech] have to have a product that is functional and will cure people," Karikó explained in 2021. "It was just so much better than a paper, then another paper that maybe nobody would read."

mRNA Vaccine in Mice and Monkeys

Perhaps Karikó was recalling the lack of peer interest in the pioneering paper that she and Weissman had published in 2005. But she had not completely given up on publications, writing a comprehensive review of mRNA technologies and treatments with Şahin and Türeci. Their 2014 paper discussed "key challenges and opportunities in developing [such therapies] into a new class of drugs."

Karikó continued to uphold a research partnership, albeit long distance, with Weissman, which also led to publications. Together with Norbert Pardi, a Hungarian scientist whom Karikó had earlier invited to work with her in Pennsylvania, and a number of other researchers, she tested a modified mRNA vaccine for the Zika virus on mice and monkeys. In 2017 their results appeared in a landmark paper on the success of mRNA vaccines against the Zika virus. Published in the prestigious journal *Nature*, the paper explained how several groups of mice were injected intradermally (below the skin) with an mRNA Zika vaccine. Several groups of unvaccinated mice served as controls.

Two weeks later, all the mice were injected intravenously (directly into a vein) with the Zika virus. Blood samples were taken from the mice after three days. Although most of the unvaccinated

Becoming infected with the Zika virus during pregnancy can result in the baby developing microcephaly, a condition that causes the brain and cranium of the skull to be much smaller than normal. It is often accompanied with other, potentially life-threatening, conditions. With proper care, however, many people with microcephaly can live full lives.

mice had the virus in their blood, those that had been inoculated were virus-free. After twenty weeks, another set of blood tests was performed. Again, the control mice had the virus and the vaccinated mice did not. These results also held true for identical experiments done with monkeys. While the control monkeys' blood was infected with Zika, the vaccinated monkeys were protected with only one immunized animal showing a very low level of the virus. Karikó could be proud of what she and her colleagues had accomplished. Their paper was the first to present strong evidence that mRNA vaccines were effective in preventing disease.

A Sudden Threat

Karikó was visiting her sister in Hungary in early 2020 when alarming reports reached her. Several dozen residents of Wuhan, China, had become ill with an unknown respiratory disease. No one knew the cause, though some of the cases seemed to be linked to an outbreak at a large seafood market. Patients experienced fever, chills, body aches, severe coughs, and breathing problems. On January 11, China reported the first known death from the mysterious pneumonia, a sixty-one-year-old man who shopped regularly at the Wuhan market. Soon after the first cases appeared, scientists in China identified the cause of the illness as a coronavirus related to the one that causes severe acute respiratory syndrome (SARS). Even as she thought about what could cause such an outbreak, Karikó didn't believe at first that the virus would travel over 4,000 miles (6,437 km) to Hungary, let alone nearly 7,000 miles (11,265 km) to the United States.

Şahin soon changed her mind. Unlike Karikó, he suspected the disease would spread to other countries and perhaps around the world. He backed up his worries with some quick research and math calculations: Wuhan's population numbered at least eleven million, and twenty-three hundred flights took off from its airport each week, many to international destinations. Estimating that each person with the virus would transmit it to at least several others, Şahin put the mortality rate at between 0.3 and 10. This meant that up to ten patients could die for every hundred stricken with the disease. According to Şahin's analysis, at least two million people could die. This was a far greater death toll than any pandemic in recent times. Less than two weeks after China reported the first death, cases were confirmed in Japan, Thailand, and South Korea. The first known case in the United States was announced on January 21. The patient, a man in his thirties, had visited Wuhan.

BioNTech specialized in cancer treatments rather than infectious disease such as the virus spreading through Wuhan and beyond. But Şahin believed he could create a safe and effective vaccine and decided to channel all of BioNTech's resources to

Many Kinds of Coronavirus

Hundreds of viruses fall into the category of coronaviruses. Most only affect a particular species of animal, such as bats or chickens. When a virus mutates, it sometimes gains the ability to infect a different species as well. Then a coronavirus that started out in cats or bats could possibly infect a human, who could then pass it on to other humans.

In 1964 June Almeida, a pioneering virology researcher, identified and helped name the first coronaviruses to affect humans. As of 2022, seven coronaviruses have been found to make humans sick. Four are relatively harmless, causing an illness such as the common cold. Three cause much more serious illness. One coronavirus illness, SARS, was identified in 2003. The most prominent symptoms include sore throat, fever, cough, and muscle ache. In twelve years 8,098 people contracted the disease and 774 people died. Another coronavirus causes Middle East respiratory syndrome (MERS), which had outbreaks in 2012, 2015, and 2018. Patients experienced shortness of breath, cough, and fever. MERS was often fatal. These virus outbreaks affected almost no one in the United States.

On February 11, 2020, the World Health Organization (WHO) gave an official name to the new rapidly spreading virus. It is the second coronavirus that causes severe acute respiratory syndrome, and so it was named SARS-CoV-2.

In their labeling, scientists have drawn a distinction between the virus and the disease that it causes. The disease caused by SARS-CoV-2, COVID-19, is named from the beginning letters of *coronavirus disease* and the last two digits of 2019, the year the disease emerged. As of November 2022, over 635 million cases of COVID-19 had been reported globally with over 6.5 million deaths.

that end. Telling his employees to cancel any vacation plans, he launched Project Lightspeed to develop, test, and produce a vaccine that would be different in principle from any previous one. Karikó was impressed with her boss's determination to help treat this mysterious illness. "He's a visionary," Karikó told the *Pennsylvania Gazette*, "and he immediately thought, 'Oh, we need to do something with that.'"

The First Inoculation

Eighteenth-century British doctor Edward Jenner is credited with administering the first successful vaccine. In 1796 he came upon a milkmaid with pus-filled sores on her skin. This indicated that the young woman had the disease known as cowpox, a relatively mild illness that passes from cows to humans. Throughout the countryside, stories circulated that people who had cowpox never contracted the much more serious, sometimes deadly ailment smallpox. If true, Jenner reasoned, perhaps the intentional exposure to cowpox from one person to another could spread that protection against smallpox. To test his theory, Jenner took some material from the young girl's sores and placed it in contact with two small cuts he made in the arm of eight-year-old James Phipps, the son of his gardener.

The boy became mildly ill but recovered within two weeks. He was safe from cowpox, but what about smallpox? Risking the child's health and life, Jenner inoculated him again, this time with material from smallpox pustules. When the boy remained well, Jenner concluded that his experiment had worked. James's inoculation with cowpox had prevented him from getting the more serious disease. But Jenner was not finished with James. He inoculated the child with the disease twenty times. Fortunately, James remained well, and Jenner went on to test the procedure on other subjects.

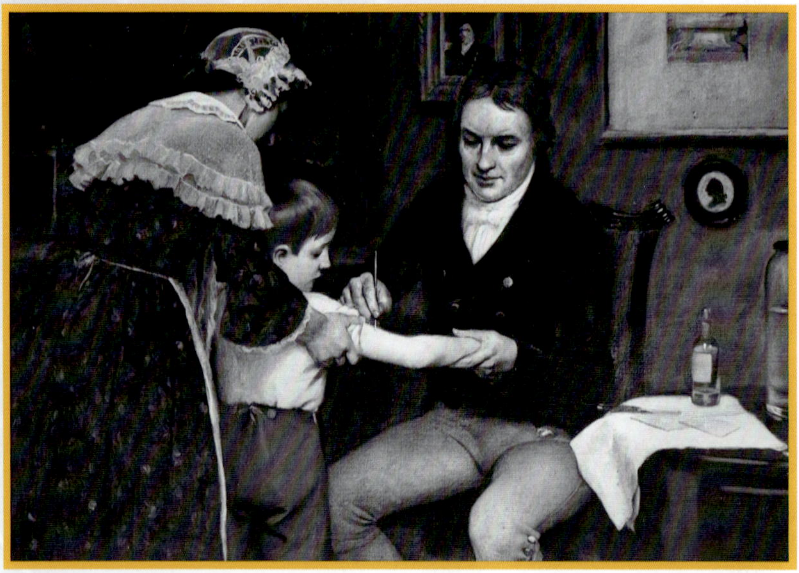

This painting shows Edward Jenner performing the first vaccination against smallpox on James Phipps.

James Phipps was not the first person to be inoculated with cowpox, but Jenner was the first to publish his findings, and so his is the name remembered. Although James would have had little or no say in participating in the experiment, Jenner never forgot the debt he owed the first person he had vaccinated. Years later, when James was married and the father of two children, Jenner gave him a free lease on a comfortable cottage.

Modern Vaccines

By the twenty-first century, scientists had developed several types of vaccines that protect against contagious diseases. To confer immunity, a vaccine may use one of the following: a live-attenuated, or weakened, version of the virus that is no longer able to cause serious illness; a killed or inactive virus that cannot infect cells; a part of the virus or bacteria such as a protein; or a toxin that is produced by a bacterium.

Before Vaccines: Variolation

As a young woman in early eighteenth-century England, Lady Mary Montagu contracted a severe case of smallpox. Despite the dire predictions of her doctors, Montagu recovered, though scarred by the disease. A year after her illness, Montagu and her young son accompanied her husband to Constantinople in the Ottoman Empire (present-day Istanbul, Turkey) where he was the British ambassador. Montagu soon learned of the practice in which elderly ladies used needles to insert smallpox material under the skin of their clients. The resulting illness was generally milder than when the disease was contracted normally. Montagu was so impressed with the technique that she arranged for her three-year-old son to undergo inoculation before the family's return to England, where the child would have greater exposure to the disease.

Although Montagu hoped to introduce the technique after the family arrived home, the physicians of her day were not inclined to listen to a woman advocating a procedure from a non-Christian country. But a smallpox epidemic in London in 1721 prompted her to have her second child, a little girl, inoculated, this time in the presence of King George I's doctor. The child's rapid recovery convinced many of her friends to have their children vaccinated too. Although the procedure, known as variolation, posed health risks, it was usually not as dangerous as getting the virus naturally. By the end of the eighteenth century, the practice had spread throughout Europe and to North America.

After the vaccine is injected into the body, the immune system recognizes a foreign intruder and mounts a defense. Usually it takes a few weeks to produce antibodies to a virus. After that, any reappearance of the virus in a person's body stimulates the immune system to create more antibodies and lymphocytes (white blood cells that fight infection as B and T cells do), and the person should not feel any serious symptoms of the disease.

Typically, vaccines take ten to fifteen years to develop and test. But outbreaks of previously unknown diseases, with the potential to infect thousands globally, demand faster results. In 2013 an epidemic of Ebola, an extremely serious viral disease that causes fever and internal bleeding, broke out in western Africa,

An outbreak of Ebola in the Democratic Republic of the Congo was partially contained due to the introduction of vaccines against the virus. The vaccines are still undergoing clinical trials, but have been shown to be safe and protective, so the World Health Organization approved them for the most at-risk individuals. By June 2020, over three hundred thousand people had been vaccinated.

Lipid Nanoparticles: The Essential Vehicle

Karikó and Weissman knew that a specialized delivery system would be required to use mRNA therapeutically. The fragile mRNA molecules had to be protected from disintegrating before they entered the cells. Then they had to be incorporated into the cytoplasm. The essential vehicle proved to be lipid nanoparticles, tiny bubbles of fat between 100 and 400 nanometers in size. A nanometer is one billionth of a meter. About one hundred thousand nanometers make up the thickness of a sheet of paper.

In the 1990s, Pieter Cullis and his team at the University of British Columbia in Vancouver, Canada, had made a major advance in encapsulating large molecules, such as mRNA, into the fatty bubbles. They manipulated the surface of the nanoparticles so that they fused with the cell membranes they encountered, thereby safely delivering mRNA into the cytoplasm. A team led by biochemist Ian MacLachlan went on to develop the technology further in ways that allowed pharmaceutical companies to create more specialized lipid nanoparticles and keep the genetic material they transported safer. During the COVID pandemic, Cullis helped pharmaceutical companies package mRNA shots in lipid nanoparticles. "It's all a bit surreal to be involved in something as big as this," Cullis said in 2022. He stressed that the COVID vaccine is "really the product of the work of hundreds of people."

prompting a swift and urgent response. With the investment of hundreds of millions of dollars and the commitment of scientists on three continents, researchers developed a vaccine for Ebola in just five years. When an outbreak occurred in the Democratic Republic of the Congo in 2018, over three thousand people received the vaccine, helping to stem the epidemic quickly.

SIX KINDS OF VACCINES

Vaccines can be divided into several types, depending on the material they use to confer immunity. Each has its own strengths and drawbacks.

TYPES OF VACCINES

TYPE	PLUSES	MINUSES	EXAMPLES
Live-attenuated vaccines: use a weakened version of a virus to confer immunity	Strong, long-lasting immunity; few, if any, booster shots needed	Extremely small chance that the virus could cause a mild case of the disease it is meant to prevent	Measles, chickenpox, oral polio vaccine (no longer used in the United States)
Subunit vaccines: use pieces of a virus or bacteria, such as a protein, sugar molecule, or casing to confer immunity	Provide strong immunity; no risk to persons with compromised immune systems	Booster shots required	Whooping cough, pneumonia, shingles
Toxoid vaccines: use an inactivated toxin, a harmful substance made by a bacteria or virus, to confer immunity	Stable and long-lasting; cannot cause the disease or spread to unvaccinated people	May cause local reaction at the injection site	Diphtheria, tetanus

Note: According to the CDC, "Any vaccine can cause side effects. For the most part these are minor (for example a sore arm or low-grade fever) and go away within a few days." Side effects of the mRNA COVID-19 vaccine also tend to be mild and similar to the side effects of other common vaccines, including the influenza and tetanus vaccines. In rare cases, the COVID-19 vaccine causes pericarditis (inflammation of the membrane surrounding the heart) and myocarditis (inflammation of the heart muscle). But most people recover quickly with medical care.

TYPES OF VACCINES (continued)

TYPE	PLUSES	MINUSES	EXAMPLES
Inactivated vaccines: use killed virus to confer immunity	No chance of causing the disease	Booster shots often required	Hepatitis A, influenza, Salk polio vaccine
Viral vector vaccines: use a modified virus (vector) to deliver an antigen (a toxin or foreign substance from a different virus) to confer immunity on that different virus	Provide strong immunity	Previous exposure to the vector could weaken the immunity	Ebola, Janssen (Johnson & Johnson) COVID-19
Messenger RNA (mRNA) vaccines: use synthetic mRNA to deliver instructions to cells for making a protein that will provoke an immune response to a disease	Can be developed quickly; can be easily modified to target variants to a disease; no possibility of the vaccine causing the disease	Booster shots required	Moderna and Pfizer-BioNTech COVID-19

A more serious outbreak in 2019 convinced hundreds of thousands of people to get vaccinated, saving many lives. The vaccination of more than forty thousand people in 2020 brought yet another outbreak of Ebola under control.

The much larger threat of a global pandemic from the new coronavirus disease in 2020 meant that even five years was too long to wait for a vaccine. Like Karikó and Weissman, Şahin realized that mRNA could provide a vital shortcut in the way vaccines were made. Millions of lives were at risk.

How mRNA Vaccines Work

Synthetic messenger RNA, as developed by Karikó and Weissman, offered an alternative to the way traditional vaccines worked. Instead of a live or killed virus, a part of a virus, or a toxin, mRNA itself would be included in the vaccine. The mRNA would carry

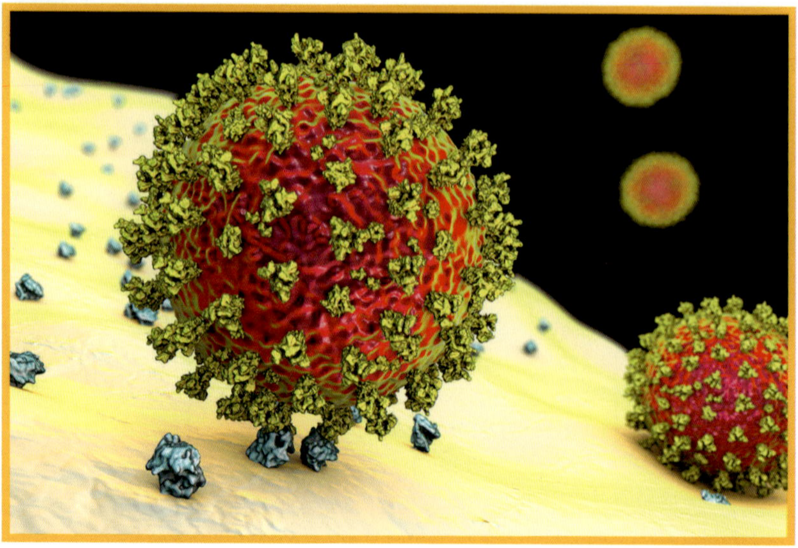

Unless stopped by an immune response, the spike proteins on the surface of COVID cells latch onto healthy host cells. The virus is then able to infect the host cells and spread.

Stabilizing the Spike Protein

When it comes to developing a vaccine, the coronavirus is a slippery target. That is because the spike protein on the coronavirus surface is not stable. It has one shape before it merges with a cell in the body and a different shape after it has infected the cell. For a vaccine to produce effective antibodies, the protein needed to be stabilized in a single configuration. Otherwise, the immune system would not be able to recognize the correct target.

Luckily, Barney Graham, then deputy director of the Vaccine Research Center at the National Institute of Allergy and Infectious Diseases, had studied the respiratory syncytial virus, which had the same tendency to change shape, and discovered a way to inhibit these changes. Several years later, when Graham learned of the mysterious pneumonia-like illness afflicting people in Wuhan, he called his former collaborator, Jason McLellan of the University of Texas. "We need to get back in the saddle," he said. "This is our time." The two men mapped out the structure of the virus's spike protein and published a technique to keep it from changing its shape in the cells. Their work enabled several drug companies, including BioNTech, Pfizer, Moderna, and Johnson & Johnson to create safe, effective COVID-19 vaccines.

Graham believes it is important to develop prototype vaccines for the major categories of viruses known to affect humans. In the event of a future viral pandemic, the appropriate prototype could be modified or adapted to produce a vaccine against a mutated form of the virus. Graham is also extremely concerned about vaccine equity. He wants to ensure that people of all nationalities, races, and socioeconomic backgrounds have the same access to lifesaving vaccines.

instructions for manufacturing the spike protein that characterizes the coronavirus. Because this protein studs the surface of the virus like miniscule spikes, it gives the virus a slight resemblance to a crown—hence the name coronavirus. *Corona* comes from the Latin word for crown.

The big hurdle in creating a traditional vaccine is growing the coronavirus in culture dishes and isolating the spike protein. Messenger RNA vaccines eliminate weeks or months from the process. Instead of delivering the actual spike protein into the body, mRNA vaccines for COVID deliver the instructions for making it. Then the body's cells make the spike protein, the mRNA breaks down, and the immune system responds to protect the body from developing the illness in a future exposure.

"Just a Technical Thing"

Although many companies would focus on creating a COVID vaccine in the early months of 2020, only BioNTech (in 2018) and Moderna (in 2017) had licensed the patent that allowed them to use Karikó and Weissman's mRNA technology. The task of these two companies was to develop the instructions for protein creation that the mRNA would take into the cells. To do this, scientists needed to know the virus's genome—that is, its complete set of genes. Since the outbreak was new and still mostly confined to China, scientists in other countries hadn't had the chance to study the virus as thoroughly. Only when the virus's genome was published on the internet in January 2020 were BioNTech and Moderna able to move forward with mRNA vaccines. Once that information appeared online, everything moved with astonishing speed. "I think we can build a vaccine quickly," Şahin told Türeci. "We have to contribute." After downloading the virus's genome, Şahin developed eight possible patterns for a vaccine in less than two days. These vaccine candidates each had a different design and molecular target. Some would be better than others in developing antibodies, but Şahin couldn't tell yet which ones would prove most effective.

Karikó, in an interview with *Scientific American*, offered one reason why work on the vaccine proceeded so rapidly. "From 2018 we [at BioNTech] had worked with Pfizer [another biotechnology company] to develop a vaccine for influenza. And we were all ready to start a clinical trial for that. But switching over to COVID, it was just a technical thing." The instructions in the synthetic mRNA to make an influenza particle simply had to be replaced with directions for the coronavirus spike protein.

But developing the vaccine was only the first step. The vaccine could not be made available to the general public until it underwent a series of very stringent clinical trials, in which the vaccine would be given to humans for the first time. As she carefully followed each stage of the trials, Karikó remained confident of a positive outcome. At the University of Pennsylvania, she had helped create mRNA vaccines for other illnesses, including the Zika virus, HIV, and influenza, and tested them, with great success, on animals. "I was aware that [mRNA] is a very good way to make a vaccine," she told *Scientific American* in 2021. "It was already demonstrated in animal studies that it is such an excellent vaccine." Confidently, she waited for the results of the clinical trials. The stakes couldn't have been higher.

Zhang Yongzhen: "It Was Very Dangerous"

On January 3, 2020, Dr. Zhang Yongzhen received a small metal box with respiratory samples from seven patients who had contracted the strange new virus in Wuhan. Zhang and his colleagues at the Shanghai Public Health Clinical Center in China set to work immediately. They had to isolate the virus from human genes and from organisms and bacteria often found in the human mouth. Then they worked around the clock for two days to identify the genetic sequence of the virus. "It took us less than forty hours, so very, very fast," Zhang told *Time* magazine. "Then I realized that this virus is closely related to SARS, probably 80 [percent]. So certainly, it was very dangerous."

Zhang explained the gravity of the situation to China's National Health Commission. Realizing the importance of sharing the genome with the rest of the world, Zhang submitted his information to the GenBank of the US National Center for Biotechnology Information. But his work remained stalled there, pending a review that might not take place for days or weeks.

Less than a week after completing the virus gene sequence, Zhang was in a plane about to take off from the Shanghai airport when his cell phone rang. Zhang's colleague, Eddie Holmes from Melbourne, Australia, knew Zhang had sequenced the virus and implored his friend to make the genome available at once. He underscored the urgency by mentioning the growing number of cases in Wuhan and the new cases appearing in Hong Kong. Researchers needed the genome to develop test kits and vaccines. "Can you release it?" Holmes asked. "You need to release it to me."

Zhang knew China's Ministry of Health had issued an order prohibiting the publication of the genome. He also knew that other government labs had sequenced the virus and withheld their results. If he complied with Holmes's request, Zhang might be seen as challenging the government's edict. "I asked Eddie to give me one minute to think," Zhang recalled more than six months later. "Then I said ok." By the time Zhang arrived in Beijing, the results had been posted on virological.org, and scientists all over the world were downloading the sequence.

Although Zhang's lab was investigated by authorities, he denies reports that he suffered serious repercussions as a result of his action. He continued to work diligently, screening viral samples in the early months of the pandemic. On October 26, 2020, he received an award for "outstanding data sharing" at the International Conference on Genomics in Wuhan.

This security guard stands in front of building A3 of the Shanghai Public Clinical Center, where COVID patients are quarantined, in Shanghai, China, on February 17, 2020.

CHAPTER 7

PANDEMIC

The coronavirus spread with extraordinary speed. By February 2020, more than twenty-one hundred people had died from COVID-19. Most of the deaths occurred in mainland China, but health professionals knew that the virus could not be contained. Countries began to restrict travel to stop the rate of infection. On March 11, WHO declared COVID-19 a global pandemic. Almost no place on Earth was safe from the deadly surge of the virus.

Still based in Germany, Karikó pursued her demanding work schedule. The general air of uncertainty and anxiety spurred by the pandemic made it a terrible time to be separated from her family. On March 13, she boarded a plane for the United States to be with her husband on his birthday. She didn't realize that stringent travel regulations were about to be implemented. Her flight was the last to enter the country before severe lockdown measures began. Karikó would spend the rest of the year in Philadelphia, working and monitoring progress on the vaccine from home.

Rising at 5 a.m., she began her day with a good workout on her rowing machine. Physical exercise was a way to challenge herself and keep physically and mentally alert. Afterward, she stationed herself in front of her computer to advise her team over video calls about protocols and techniques. Because BioNTech was a small company that lacked the capability to produce massive amounts of vaccine for large-scale testing, it teamed up with the well-established drug company, Pfizer, to handle the logistics.

Less than two weeks after Karikó's arrival in the United States, the Centers for Disease Control and Prevention (CDC) reported 82,174 cases of COVID-19 nationwide. According to the WHO, the country had surpassed both China and Italy in the number of cases and was on target to become the new epicenter of the pandemic.

During the COVID-19 pandemic, a new acronym became popular: PPE, standing for personal protective equipment. Health-care professionals need PPE to protect themselves against the virus while treating sick patients.

New York City was especially hit hard. Hospitals were overcrowded, and there were not enough ventilators (breathing machines) to meet the needs of dangerously ill patients. The city's morgues could not handle the number of deceased patients. Refrigerated trucks were parked outside hospitals to hold the bodies.

In the midst of the growing crisis, clinical trials of the coronavirus vaccines developed by biotechnology companies proceeded as rapidly as possible. Held to a very high standard, clinical trials have to pass three distinct phases to prove the safety and efficacy of a vaccine before it can be submitted to the FDA for approval. With the death toll from COVID-19 mounting, time was critical. To speed the process, BioNTech tested multiple vaccine candidates at once, and at times trials in each of the phases occurred simultaneously.

Phase 1 Trials

The goal of a phase 1 trial is to determine the right dosage, or amount, of the vaccine to be included in each shot. At this point, the trials don't determine the extent to which the vaccine is effective, but rather they have to show that the immune system has been stimulated. The first volunteers, called participants, in phase 1 studies are given very small doses, and the doctors, called investigators, monitor them carefully for signs of side effects and the responses of antibodies and T cells. If all goes well, another group of participants receives a bigger dose of the vaccine and their bodies' reactions are observed. Phase 1 trials continue with ever-increasing doses until the investigators have determined that the vaccine is safe and that it affects the immune system. If the vaccine fails to meet these goals, it must be discontinued. BioNTech tested several vaccine candidates for COVID-19 in phase 1 to determine which provoked the best immune response without causing serious adverse effects.

Phase 2 Trials

Once a vaccine has completed its phase 1 trials and been selected from among the various candidates, phase 2 trials, with more participants, usually begin. During phase 2 of testing the Pfizer-BioNTech vaccine, Karikó kept track of the different combinations that were tested. Some of the several hundred participants received a single dose of the vaccine. Others received two smaller doses of the vaccine, three or six weeks apart. The researchers measured the antibodies in the blood of each participant to see which dosage and vaccination schedule produced the best results.

Phase 3 Trials

Like all her colleagues, Karikó was getting increasingly excited as phase 3 trials began on July 27, 2020. Thousands of participants from across the globe would be involved, as well as hundreds of investigators to monitor the participants' health and side effects. The participants were divided into a test group, which received the vaccine, and a control group, which received a placebo, an ineffective but harmless substance. Giving some participants a placebo allows researchers to compare the two groups and verify that the vaccine worked in the test group. The participants in the two groups were fairly evenly matched in age, gender, ethnicity, and overall health. Neither the participants nor the investigators were told who got the vaccine and who got the placebo, making the trial a double-blind study. This precaution eliminates bias and prevents preconceived ideas by the investigators from inadvertently affecting their evaluation of the results.

During their daily lives, some of the participants in a drug trial will inevitably contract the infectious disease being studied. Once the number of cases hits a predetermined number, trial records are checked to see who got the drug and who got the placebo. This is called unblinding the study. Generally, it takes a year, several years,

Diversity in Clinical Trials

As the Pfizer-BioNTech vaccine moved into phase 3 trials, Şahin and Pfizer CEO Albert Bourla discussed the need for diversity among the participants. In the past, people of color and women had not been proportionally represented in—or even excluded from—clinical trials. According to Bourla in his book *Moonshot*, Black Americans generally comprise only 5 percent of participants in clinical trials, although they make up about 13 percent of the population. The statistics were even worse for persons of Latin American origin, who make up 19 percent of the US population but only 1 percent of those participating in clinical studies. Pfizer strived to surpass these numbers. With the COVID-19 trials, it was more critical than ever to have a significantly diverse number of participants. Researchers had to make sure that the vaccine was safe and effective for all people. And a diverse test group would encourage people of all racial and ethnic backgrounds to trust the vaccine and to get inoculated after it was approved by the FDA.

BioNTech and Pfizer actively sought Black Americans, members of the Navajo Nation, and members of Hispanic or Latinx communities to participate in their clinical trials. Roughly 42 percent of global participants and 30 percent of those from the United States came from usually underrepresented racial, geographic, and age groups.

or even longer to reach the set number of cases required to unblind the study. This slows down the evaluation and the final approval of the drug or vaccine.

The process moved much more rapidly with the COVID-19 vaccine. The pandemic raged so uncontrollably that by November enough participants from the global phase 3 clinical trial had been infected with the disease that the investigators unblinded the study. The researchers could then determine how many participants from each group got COVID-19. By comparing the number of COVID-19 cases between the two groups, researchers could determine how effective the vaccine was at preventing the disease. If most of the COVID-19 cases came from the control group, and very few cases came from the test group, that would indicate that the vaccine protected members of the test group when they were exposed to the virus.

"We Will Get through This"

As clinical tests moved forward through 2020, most people around the world had to greatly alter their lives to avoid getting sick. In the US, the CDC recommended people follow ever-changing health guidelines to prevent the spread of the coronavirus. Social distancing, the practice of maintaining a physical distance between oneself and others, hindered large gatherings and even family get-togethers. Individuals wore surgical masks to capture respiratory droplets from their noses and mouths as they went to the grocery store or did other essential errands, protecting those around them as well as themselves from a potential infection. Since many people ventured from home only when necessary, businesses suffered, especially small establishments that required customers to remain indoors in an enclosed area for long periods, such as restaurants, beauty salons, and movie theaters. Transportation and the travel and tourism industries saw a steep decline in profits. By May 20, 2020, around eighteen million people in the United States had been temporarily laid off and were unemployed, with low-income and minority workers hit the hardest.

Concerts and athletic events were canceled. Many colleges and schools closed, switching from in-person to online classes. Children sometimes had difficulty adjusting to "virtual learning" and did not

Many businesses started more rigorous sanitation practices, such as disinfecting surfaces that many people may come in contact with, including grocery carts.

do as well as they had when attending school in person. Parents whose jobs did not permit them to work at home struggled to find proper supervision for their young children. As early as March 2020, people were already experiencing the pandemic as a major tragedy and could only speculate as to when a vaccine would be available.

"People are feeling like this is never going to come to an end," NIH then director Francis Collins told Fauci, then the director of the National Institute of Allergy and Infectious Diseases, in an informal interview.

A familiar face to Americans from his frequent appearances as part of the White House Coronavirus Task Force, Fauci was hailed by many as "the scientific voice of reason."

Collins continued, "The uncertainty and anxiety is weighing on people. And many people have seen loved ones fall ill, or even die. . . . And some people are wondering: Are we going to get through this?"

Operation Warp Speed

Although he sometimes played down the dangers of the pandemic, then president of the United States Donald Trump understood the urgent need for a vaccine. On May 15, 2020, he announced a program to advance the simultaneous production of various vaccines that depended on different types of medical technologies and that were being developed by different companies. The $10 billion program was originally dubbed Operation Warp Speed, from the television show *Star Trek*'s term for travel surpassing the speed of light. According to the fact sheet published by the Department of Health and Human Services, Operation Warp Speed "aimed to produce and deliver 300 million doses of safe and effective vaccines with the initial doses available by January 2021."

Pfizer did not take funds directly from Operation Warp Speed, but the company accepted the program's deal for the US government to buy one hundred million doses of its vaccine (about $2 billion worth) as soon as the FDA approved it. The guaranteed sales helped give BioNTech, Pfizer, and other companies the financial security to forge rapidly ahead on the vaccine.

Most experts credit Operation Warp Speed with contributing significantly to the rapid development of safe, successful vaccines. "[Operation Warp Speed] is a bright spot in the pandemic response," said Jesse Goodman, former head scientist of the FDA.

Tinglong Dai of Johns Hopkins University agrees. "You can like or hate the Trump administration," he told CBC News in 2020, "but no doubt [Operation Warp Speed is] a huge success, unprecedented success."

"We will get through this for absolutely certain," replied Fauci. "Science will get us through this. We will get a vaccine. . . . So the only message that I think we can jointly tell the American public and the global public is that we will get through this. Hang in there. It will end, we promise you."

Joyful Interlude

Focused on that promise of a vaccine to end the pandemic, Karikó continued to spend long hours in front of her computer conversing with colleagues. Although her name wasn't in the headlines, she kept abreast on everything that was happening with her research group at BioNTech and eagerly awaited results. Meanwhile, exciting things were happening in her family. Her daughter was getting married in October, the same month that Karikó and Francia would celebrate their own fortieth anniversary.

Her daughter's wedding in Virginia provided Karikó with a welcome respite from a heavy work schedule and from the bleak news of the pandemic. But Francia knew Karikó's work was always in the back of her mind. After the ceremony, she and her husband made a speech in honor of the young couple. Francia joked that Karikó would be happy to respond if anyone had a question about the vaccine. Everyone laughed.

"I Knew It"

Upon returning to Philadelphia after the wedding, Karikó knew it wouldn't be long until the results of the clinical trials were in. Tense with anticipation, she continued her daily routine of early morning exercise followed by hours of reviewing reports from BioNTech. "Watch the news today," she would tell her daughter during their frequent phone calls. "Tomorrow, as soon as you wake up, Google search: BioNTech." Days and weeks passed without any news.

Finally, on November 8, mere days after the election of President Joe Biden, Karikó received the call she had been waiting for. The Pfizer-BioNTech vaccine was more than 90 percent effective in preventing COVID-19, surpassing the expectations of many scientists. As eagerly as she had anticipated the moment, Karikó found herself unprepared for the sudden surge of emotion she experienced. She had been right all along. mRNA was a tremendous therapeutic tool. "I started to breathe very hard," Karikó later recalled. "I was so excited that I was afraid of dying or something." But Karikó pulled herself together quickly. By the time the call was over, she could turn to her husband and say matter-of-factly, "Oh, it works. I knew it would."

A woman of simple tastes, Karikó celebrated the success of the vaccine by treating herself to Goobers, a brand of chocolate-covered peanuts. Usually she restricted her portions. "Today," she told her husband, "I'm going to eat the whole [box]."

Anthony Fauci: "And That's It"

Long before he became a familiar face through then president Trump's press briefing on COVID-19, Anthony Fauci had made important contributions to public health. As the head of the National Institute of Allergy and Infectious Diseases, he saw the country through outbreaks of serious illnesses, including AIDS, SARS, swine flu, Zika, and Ebola. Criticized severely in the late 1980s by ACT UP, an organization primarily of LGBTQ+ activists who demanded faster help in treating patients with AIDS, Fauci listened to their stories carefully. He invited protesters at the NIH to meet with him in his office, and he traveled to New York and San Francisco to meet with other activists.

ACT UP protesters stage a die-in, a form of protest in which the participants simulate being dead and use slogans on signs or clothing to explain why they "died," on the front steps of the FDA headquarters in Rockville, Maryland, in 1988.

Members of the LGBTQ+ community were angry because AIDS patients had no access to experimental drugs that were their only hope against a fatal disease. Fauci helped change that by supporting a proposal called parallel track, which granted patients access to drugs that were still unapproved by the FDA but proved to be safe. He established a division at the NIH focused on finding a cure for AIDS. Fauci's openness to patients' demands helped bring about what has been called "a revolution in American medicine." Rather than defer submissively to doctors, patients began to educate themselves and participate more fully in medical decisions.

Thrust into the national spotlight by the coronavirus, Fauci told Americans what to expect and how to protect themselves as the pandemic unfolded. At times this meant contradicting Trump's overly optimistic views. But throughout a career that included advising both Republican and Democratic presidents, he maintained his political neutrality. "You stay completely apolitical and non-ideological," he has stated, "and you stick to what you do. I'm a scientist and I'm a physician. And that's it." In December 2022, Fauci retired from the NIH but told the *New York Times* that he intends to keep working. His future plans include giving talks, writing a memoir, and encouraging young people who are interested in science, medicine, and public service. On July 1, 2023, Fauci began a new position as a professor at Georgetown University's School of Medicine and at the university's McCourt School of Public Policy. His specialty is in the school's division of infectious diseases, which treats patients, conducts research, and mentors future physicians in the field.

CHAPTER

8

A FUTURE WIDE OPEN

The day after Karikó received that momentous phone call, Pfizer announced the preliminary outcome of its clinical trials. "Today is a great day for science and humanity," declared Bourla, chair and CEO of Pfizer.

Şahin also issued a statement. "When we embarked on this journey ten months ago, this is what we aspired to achieve," he said. He spoke of the vaccine as a "milestone on our path towards ending this pandemic and for all of us to regain a sense of normality."

Emergency Authorization

On December 11, 2020, the FDA issued an EUA for the Pfizer-BioNTech vaccine. Seven days later, Moderna also received an EUA for its COVID-19 vaccine. The early permission to begin inoculation reflected the agency's determination that "the known and potential benefits outweigh the known and potential risks of the vaccine." Speed was imperative if the disease were to be defeated. A second overwhelming surge of the virus was challenging the capacity of hospitals in the United States. More than 226,000 cases had been reported. Governors would determine the distributions of each state's supply of vaccine, but recommendations from the Advisory Committee on Immunization Practices (part of the CDC) called for health-care workers and residents of long-term living facilities such as nursing homes and assisted-living communities to receive the first shots. Full immunization consisted of two shots scheduled twenty-one to twenty-eight days apart.

"People's Concerns Need to Be Taken Very Seriously"

One week after the EUA had been approved, Karikó and Weissman received their own injections. Years of persistence in the face of discouragement and rejection had paid off. Seeing health-care workers line up at the University of Pennsylvania to receive their shots and hearing the applause for herself and Weissman, Karikó knew she had finally succeeded in her goal of making a significant contribution to health care. But even as she thought back to her past struggles, she was already looking toward the future. "I'm hopeful," she said, "now that there is so much interest and excitement for this research, that it will be possible to develop and test mRNA vaccine technology for prevention and treatment of other diseases too."

As the number of people receiving the vaccine grew, so did public interest in the researchers who had worked so hard to make it available as swiftly as possible. Who had achieved this medical miracle? How had they done it? People found Karikó to be an inspiring and appealing hero. She was described as "quirky" and "cheerful" by the *New York Post*.

Sandra Lindsay: Vaccine Advocate

When critical-care nurse Sandra Lindsay learned that the COVID-19 vaccine would be available at her work the next day, she didn't have to think twice. "I was like, 'Give it to me. Give it to me now,'" she recalled in 2022. "No second thoughts. No shivers, no fears." Chosen at random from staff volunteers at Long Island Jewish Medical Center, Lindsay became the first person in the United States to receive a COVID-19 shot outside of the clinical trials. The historic moment was televised live on CNN on December 14, 2020. As a Black woman and immigrant from Jamaica, Lindsay hoped that her example would "inspire people who look like me, who are skeptical in general about taking vaccines."

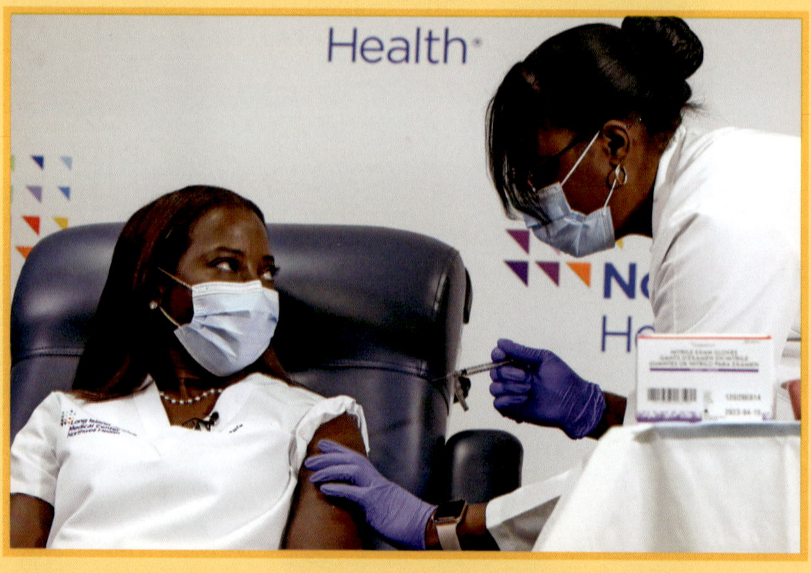

Sandra Lindsay receives her first dose of the Pfizer-BioNTech COVID-19 vaccine.

For months, Lindsay had been on the so-called front lines of the pandemic, supervising hundreds of nurses and caring for severely sick patients. "I just felt broken, defeated, just tired and burned out," she told the Associated Press one year after her first shot. "Witnessing the overwhelming loss of lives, loss of livelihoods." Lindsay dealt with her emotional pain by becoming a forceful vaccine advocate. She spoke at virtual town meetings and other events, urging people to bring their concerns to health-care professionals and to ask questions. In August 2020, she visited her native country of Jamaica and saw firsthand how badly the hospitals were overwhelmed with COVID-19 patients. On her return to New York, Lindsay arranged to have $800,000 worth of personal protective equipment and medical devices that supply extra oxygen sent to Jamaica.

Lindsay is passionately concerned with vaccine equity—the need for the vaccine to be distributed equally and fairly to people of all ethnic and socioeconomic groups. On February 23, 2022, she met with Abdulla Shahid, then president of the United Nations General Assembly, to discuss the urgent need to get the vaccine to people in underserved nations. Two days later, she addressed the members of the United Nations in a prerecorded video about the importance of distributing the vaccine fairly and equally to people of all backgrounds. She also discussed education and the mental health needs of those caring for very ill patients. Since her initial vaccination, Lindsay has completed her PhD and been honored at the White House by President Biden as an Outstanding American by Choice, an honor given to naturalized citizens. In 2022 she was chosen to be *USA Today*'s Women of the Year New York honoree.

"I like what I have and where I live and what I do," she told the newspaper. "I'm busy every day. Nothing will change."

But it was inevitable that some things would change. Karikó spent the beginning of 2021 working from her home in Philadelphia. As people clamored for the vaccine and the inoculation program went forward, more journalists asked for interviews. Karikó had never sought the limelight and had always guarded her work time carefully. She joked with reporters about the reading she should be doing instead of talking to them. But she felt it was important for researchers like herself to address public concerns about the vaccine. While some people couldn't wait to get their shots, others expressed skepticism and apprehension because of how quickly the vaccine had been produced and released. Did it really work? Was it really safe? Were corners cut in its development and testing? Karikó believed that if everyone understood the science behind the vaccine and the rigorous testing it had undergone, they would know they had nothing to fear from a COVID-19 shot. "People's concerns need to be taken very seriously," she told *Lifestyles Magazine*. "They need to be helped to make a decision. Most people [hesitant about the vaccine] are afraid due to a lack of knowledge, but are open to listening to the professionals they trust."

mRNA in the Fridge

As more and more people began to get vaccinated, the number of new cases per day dropped. International flights resumed, and cities lifted their mask mandates. The CDC issued new guidelines allowing indoor social gatherings without masks or social distancing if all the people who attended were fully vaccinated. Social distancing was still practiced in schools but was reduced from 6 to 3 feet (1.8 to 0.9 m) in elementary school, where the rate of infection was lower than in high school. By April 2021, people were able to travel with reasonable safety.

In many outbreaks of illness, scientists and medical professionals recommend that the public take measures to reach herd immunity. This means that enough people are vaccinated or otherwise immune to a disease so that it cannot spread as much or as fast through the population.

"A Different Place"

In January 2019, before the COVID-19 pandemic, the WHO listed vaccine hesitancy among the top ten dangers to world health. According to a statement released by the organization, reluctance to be vaccinated "threatens to reverse progress made in tackling vaccine-preventable diseases." The WHO also noted that a substantial rise in the number of vaccinations worldwide could save as many as 1.5 million lives each year.

The accuracy of the WHO's warning became tragically evident one year later in the midst of the COVID-19 pandemic. Despite vast numbers of vaccinations, the coronavirus continues to infect people. A number of variants have developed. Several factors have contributed to their spread, including a decrease in health precautions, such as mask wearing and social distancing. Although breakthrough cases can occur in people who have been vaccinated, the vaccine and subsequent booster shots greatly lessen the chance of severe illness and death. Israel was the first country to demonstrate the effectiveness of the vaccine by administering large numbers of vaccinations in early 2021. The number of COVID-19 cases fell sharply. Other countries were soon showing the same correlation: the more people vaccinated, the fewer the number of COVID-19 cases. Health officials coined a phrase to describe this, "pandemic of the unvaccinated," since most people who became severely ill had not received the vaccine.

Some people argue that the phrase fosters intolerance toward those who choose not to be inoculated. They also point to the many breakthrough cases contracted by individuals who did receive vaccinations. According to Dr. Günter Kampf, in a letter to the prestigious medical journal the *Lancet* in November 2021, "People who are vaccinated have a lower risk of severe disease but are still a relevant part of the pandemic. It is therefore wrong and dangerous to speak of a pandemic of the unvaccinated."

Despite high vaccination rates in the United States, with millions of people rushing to get the vaccine when it first became available, fewer people went on to receive the recommended booster shots for a variety of reasons, including the circulation of untrue statements about the vaccine. US surgeon general Vivek Hallegere Murthy, who has lost ten family members to COVID-19, believes it is crucial to set the record straight. "Addressing health misinformation is a core part of pandemic preparedness," he told NBC News in 2022. "If we don't address this crisis, we will be unable to effectively get the treatments and vaccines and help to people who need that help. And that will mean there will be needless suffering and loss of life that we've sadly seen with COVID." Well into the third year of the pandemic, the Omicron subvariant BA.5 continued to spread. In late July 2022, the US was still averaging about 130,000 cases daily. The death rate had reached about 450 per day. As of February 7, 2023, the total number of cases in the United States had reached 102,447,438 with 1,106,824 deaths.

By then, most Americans had returned to their normal activities. Children and teachers had returned to the classroom. "We know that COVID-19 is here to stay," said Greta Massetti, an epidemiologist at the CDC. But she stressed that vaccines, immunity due to previous infections, and treatments to prevent or lessen the severity of COVID-19 symptoms "have put us in a different place."

The CDC issued new, less stringent guidelines in August 2022 for dealing with COVID-19. Masks, social distancing, and quarantining after a known exposure to COVID-19 were no longer required. But those testing positive for COVID-19 should quarantine for five to ten days if they experience significant symptoms or have suppressed immune systems.

Karikó was now able to lecture at universities, attend conferences in other countries, and divide her time between Philadelphia and Mainz. As new vaccines and boosters were developed to combat emerging variants of the coronavirus, she chose to concentrate on other diseases that may be treated with mRNA therapy. "I want to focus on making RNA that encodes therapeutic proteins that will help heal wounds, scar (heal broken) bones, or that will help cure patients with cancer," she told Euronews in 2021. She hopes that ultimately mRNA will be used to treat a wide variety of illnesses and that the technology may allow patients to take greater responsibility for their own therapy. For example, when considering the chronic skin disease epidermolysis bullosa, which causes severe blisters and often affects children, Karikó offered an innovative and surprising solution when she spoke with the British newspaper the *Guardian*. "How about we make mRNA that the family can keep in the fridge?" That way, she continued, when a child's skin became raw and painful, a parent could simply take some mRNA and administer it to the affected areas. The mRNA would be coded to create a protein that initiates healing.

Game Changer

Independent care for epidermolysis bullosa patients is just one of many possible innovations looming on the horizon. According to Karikó and many other researchers, mRNA treatments will prove to be a game changer in medicine. New and effective therapies are expected to lead to healthier, longer lives. When Karikó first began researching mRNA, she compiled a list of thirty diseases she believed could be cured or alleviated through such treatments. mRNA research programs have begun to investigate some of these serious illnesses, such as cystic fibrosis (a genetic disorder that impairs the lungs and digestive system) and emphysema (a serious breathing disorder). But twenty-five items from Karikó's list remain to be explored with mRNA.

"There's no question of leaning back and quitting work," she once said. "Researchers are like rock musicians. They play as long as they can."

Stylish Grandmother

Early 2021 was an especially exciting time for Karikó as she waited to become a grandmother. In February her daughter gave birth to a boy, Alexander Bear Amos. Karikó was present to see the baby immediately. Within a week of Alexander's birth, she was walking along the beach in San Diego, California, with her daughter and new grandson.

Karikó would have loved to spend much more time with them. But as the year progressed, speaking engagements and interviews encroached more and more upon her time. She and Weissman received so many awards they could scarcely keep track of them. Inducted into the National Inventors Hall of Fame, Karikó was also selected for *Time* magazine's annual list of the one hundred most influential people in the world. The Carnegie Corporation of New York presented her with an award as one of 2021's Great Immigrants. Together, Karikó and Weissman received awards from Weissman's alma mater, Brandeis University, in conjunction with the Rosenstiel Foundation, and from Columbia University.

Some of the accolades seemed strange to Karikó. For example, *Glamour* magazine chose her as its Woman of the Year, an honor she thought of declining since she did not think of herself as a fashion leader. But her daughter talked her into it, pointing out that there were not enough female role models with scientific credentials such as hers for the young women who read the magazine. The photos and article in the magazine depicted Karikó as a stylish and dedicated scientist.

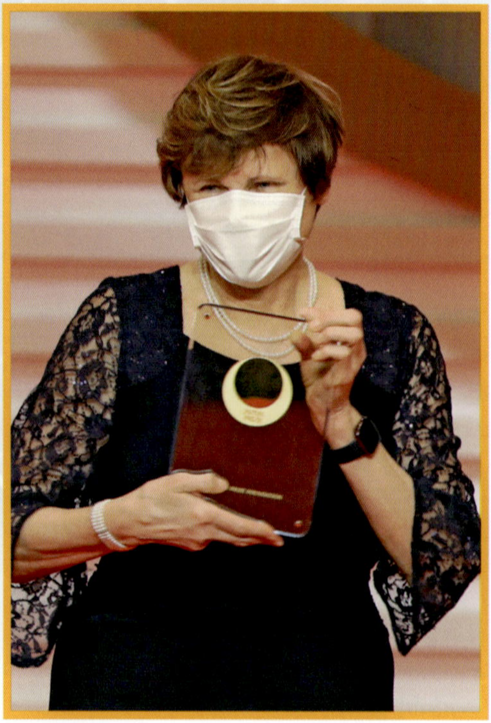

In April 2022, Karikó was awarded the Japan Prize for her work with mRNA. This international prize is awarded to scientists and researchers whose contributions to science and technology further the peace and prosperity of humankind.

Back Home in Hungary

Karikó had always made frequent trips to her home country to visit her sister and old friends, but in 2021 her family had to share her with a grateful public. Karikó's hometown of Kisújszállás and the city of Szeged welcomed her as a hero. She was asked to lecture at the prestigious General Assembly of the Hungarian Academy of Sciences. Dozens of news outlets clamored to interview her. She even met her favorite pop singer, Zorán Sztevanovity, when they were jointly interviewed on the radio. The famous musician was as happy to speak with her as she was to meet him. Sztevanovity told her that he felt honored to know that his song "Diamonds and Gold" had inspired her and helped her through difficult times. Later in September, Karikó addressed the student body at her alma mater, the University of Szeged. The students applauded enthusiastically, and the rector of the university presented her with an honorary doctorate.

"Nothing Can Generate That Kind of Feeling"

In terms of money, the biggest award that Karikó and Weissman shared (along with several other scientists) was the Breakthrough Prize, which bestows $3 million on winners in each of three categories. "I never sought any of this," Karikó told the *Philadelphia Inquirer*, expressing her surprise and gratitude. "I went forty years without any prize." Both she and Weissman said that they would use some of the prize money to further their research. She also wanted to help students with limited financial resources pursue their science education.

Varied and unexpected, honors continued to come. In addition to numerous prestigious awards from foundations and universities, Karikó has been honored by nursing homes, artists, astronomers, and more. An asteroid, 2002 AR204, is named for her, and a 220-square-foot (20 sq. m) mural in Budapest, Hungary, commemorates her lifesaving breakthrough. Meadowbrook Healthcare, a nursing facility in Plattsburgh, New York, named September 2, 2021, Katalin Karikó Appreciation Day when residents and staff wore T-shirts with her picture. They sent her a letter explaining that one week after residents received their shots, a COVID-19 outbreak occurred. Seventy individuals tested positive. As elderly people, these patients were at high risk, but thanks to the vaccine, no one became severely ill or died. On Mother's Day, residents were able to visit with children and grandchildren for the first time since the onset of the pandemic. Officials at Meadowbrook sent Karikó some photos of the event, a gesture Karikó appreciated deeply. "When you see those people, it touches you," she said later in the year. "No matter what prize you give me, nothing can generate that kind of feeling."

"I Was Curious"

At the launch of Humanitas University's eighth academic year dedicated to the medical sciences, the rector awarded the university's first honorary degree in medicine to a somewhat overwhelmed Karikó on November 29, 2021. Speaking to the students and faculty as if they were friends, Karikó expressed her excitement at receiving the award and her pleasure at exploring Milan, Italy, the site of the private university. She spoke briefly of her childhood fascinations—watching chickens hatch and cultivating plants from tiny seeds. "I was curious," she said, adding that she had great teachers.

The path from that observant little girl to a world-renowned scientist hadn't been easy, but Karikó had several life lessons to share with young people who wished to succeed in their profession. She urged them to care deeply about their work. "We spend most of our life working, so it is important to enjoy it," she said. She also emphasized the importance of dealing with stress in a positive manner and not dwelling on the things in your life that you can't control. Have faith in your abilities, she told the young people, and reach out to other students because someday you will need one another's help. She cited two instances in which students she had known at the University of Szeged helped her many years later with her research into mRNA. Getting more personal, Karikó spoke of the need to find the right life partner, as she had done. There's no need to choose between a career and a family, Karikó told the young women—surround yourself with people who will understand your ambitions and support your goals. The advice drew a round of applause. Karikó hopes and expects to see many young people of all genders make important contributions to science without sacrificing their personal lives. She ended her talk by thanking her family, colleagues, teachers, mentors, and "parents who taught me that hard work is part of life."

Emerging Variants

Over time, some viruses mutate. In the coronavirus, this means that one of the nucleotides in a gene in the spike protein is altered, creating a variant of the virus. A vaccine developed to confer immunity on the original virus may confer some immunity against a variant and lessen the severity of the illness if a vaccinated person is infected with a variant. But it will not be as effective as it is against the original virus. New vaccines need to be developed to combat emerging variants. The CDC identifies new variants by continually sequencing specimens of the virus from people who are ill. Variants are categorized by the level of risk they pose to the public. For example, Omicron was listed as a "variant of concern" in 2021 because it spread easily. A person infected with the Omicron variant could spread the disease whether or not they had symptoms or had been previously vaccinated.

This illustration depicts five variants of COVID-19. The spike proteins on the surface of each molecule are unique. As of March 2023, the CDC listed twelve variants labeled by the WHO on their website. The WHO uses a labeling system comprised of Greek letters such as alpha or beta.

Science as the Goal

In the fall of 2022, after commuting between Mainz and Philadelphia for nine years, Karikó decided to leave BioNTech to spend more time with her growing family, which includes a granddaughter born in November 2022. In keeping with family tradition, the baby, as the first girl born in her family, was named Zsuzsanna. Karikó remains a consultant for BioNTech, accepts speaking engagements, and encourages students in their pursuit of science.

Despite a demanding schedule, Karikó continues to pursue her childhood interest in plants and to share her enthusiasm on Twitter. In October 2022, she posted instructions for growing hyacinths in water culture, promising to show off her own bulbs in January. The results were stunning—colorful, flourishing blooms in the middle of winter.

"I just love my work and I continue to believe in all its possibilities," Karikó said shortly before the first COVID-19 shots were administered in the United States. "I'm just so happy to see my work bear fruit."

Karikó's optimistic view is reinforced in her dealings with students. In early 2023, she met with eight Hungarian high school students electronically from her home in Philadelphia. Each student gave a presentation on what he or she would like to do with mRNA, a vision of what might be accomplished. "They were all so inspired and talented," Karikó said. Although she could only choose four for special recognition, she told the participants that "everyone is a winner." The experience itself and the memory of what they accomplished was the reward.

Karikó advised the students to set worthwhile objectives. "The science has to be the goal," she stressed—not an academic position or awards. She also told them not to blame others when things did not work out as they hoped. Instead, they should figure out what to change in themselves.

In her own career, nothing stopped Karikó from pursuing her goals—not lack of funding, the skepticism of her colleagues, or the disappointing results of an experiment. Looking back, she sees value in the hardships she endured "because without them, I wouldn't be so tough." Profoundly grateful for Karikó and her pioneering science, people across the globe applaud the toughness, persistence, and courage that saved millions of lives.

KATALIN KARIKÓ TIMELINE

1955 Katalin Karikó is born on January 17.

1973 She begins her first year at the University of Szeged.

1980 She marries Béla Francia.

1982 She receives her PhD.

Her daughter, Zsuzsanna, who goes by Susan, is born.

1985 She loses her job at the Biological Research Centre in Szeged, immigrates to the United States, and begins working at Temple University in Philadelphia.

1989 After a year at the Naval Hospital in Bethesda, Maryland, she becomes an adjunct professor at the University of Pennsylvania.

1995 She is demoted by the University of Pennsylvania.

1998 She meets Drew Weissman.

2005 She and Weissman publish the groundbreaking paper, "Suppression of RNA Recognition by Toll-Like Receptors: The Impact of Nucleoside Modification and the Evolutionary Origin of RNA." The importance of their breakthrough is not recognized.

2006 She and Weissman launch a company, RNARx, to develop RNA treatments for diseases.

2010 RNARx does not succeed financially because Karikó and Weissman are unable to reach a licensing agreement with the University of Pennsylvania for their own synthetic mRNA.

2013 She accepts a job with BioNTech and lives most of the year in Mainz, Germany but maintains a long-distance partnership with Drew Weissman.

2020 She follows progress on the Pfizer-BioNTech COVID-19 vaccine and on the clinical trials from her home in Philadelphia.

She receives word on November 8 that the vaccine is 90 percent effective.

She and Drew Weissman receive the COVID-19 vaccine on December 18.

2021–2022 She receives numerous honors and awards, including honorary degrees from universities, and is asked to give presentations and participate in seminars.

2022 She retires from BioNTech but continues as a consultant.

2023 She continues to lecture internationally.

Her book *Breaking Through: My Life in Science* is published.

CORONAVIRUS AND PANDEMIC TIMELINE

1964 Virologist June Almeida identifies and helps name a coronavirus capable of making humans ill. (Hundreds of coronaviruses exist. Most do not affect humans).

2003 The coronavirus causing SARS is identified in China. The symptoms are similar to those of COVID-19.

2012 MERS, caused by another coronavirus, is identified in Saudi Arabia.

2020 News of an alarming illness in Wuhan, China, begins to circulate as early as January.

Gene sequencing reveals the cause is a coronavirus. Drug companies begin working on a vaccine.

The WHO names the new virus SARS-CoV-2 on February 11.

The WHO declares a global pandemic on March 11 as the disease spreads rapidly throughout the world.

The White House announces Operation Warp Speed on April 30, with a goal of three hundred million doses of COVID-19 vaccine available by January 2021.

The COVID-19 death toll in the United States surpasses two hundred thousand on September 22.

The FDA issues an emergency use authorization for the Pfizer-BioNTech vaccine on December 11 and for the Moderna vaccine on December 18.

The United States death toll from COVID-19 surpasses three hundred thousand on December 14.

Nurse Sandra Lindsay becomes the first person in the United States to receive the vaccine outside of a clinical trial on December 14.

The number of vaccinations in the United States exceeds one million on December 23.

2021 The United States COVID-19 death toll exceeds five hundred thousand on February 21.

The FDA extends the emergency use authorization for the Pfizer-BioNTech vaccine to include adolescents twelve to fifteen.

The Delta variant becomes the dominant variant in the US in June.

The WHO lists Omicron as a variant of concern on November 26.

In mid-December it becomes the dominant variant in the United States.

2022 By March 5, 56 percent of the world's population has been fully vaccinated, but the vaccine is not available in some areas.

On March 14, China institutes the zero-COVID policy, a series of lockdowns, after cases of Omicron are identified.

In mid-June, the FDA grants an emergency use authorization for the Pfizer-BioNTech vaccine for children six months to five years and for the Moderna vaccine for children six months to six years.

China lifts its strict zero-COVID policy in December.

2023 In January China announces that sixty thousand COVID-related deaths occurred in the month since its zero-COVID policy was lifted.

In January WHO director-general Dr. Tedros Adhanom Ghebreyesus says the COVID pandemic has reached a "transition point" thanks to diagnostics, treatments, and vaccines but that it remains an international emergency.

The WHO announces an end to the global COVID-19 emergency on May 5. Tedros tells reporters, "The worst thing any country could do now is to use this news as a reason to let down its guard, to dismantle the systems it has build, or to send the message to its people that COVID-19 is nothing to worry about."

GLOSSARY

acquired immunodeficiency syndrome (AIDS): a potentially life-threatening disease that severely damages the body's immune system, decreasing its ability to fight disease or infection

amino acid: an organic compound consisting of molecules that combine to create proteins

antibody: a blood protein produced to destroy a foreign substance, such as bacteria or a virus

antigen: a foreign substance that provokes the body's immune system to produce antibodies

bacteria: single-celled organisms that live in diverse environments, including the human body. Although many bacteria are beneficial, some cause disease.

B cell: a white blood cell that responds to a specific foreign substance by creating antibodies

biochemistry: the branch of science that deals with the chemistry of living things

biotechnology: the science of adapting biological systems or processes to create products, promote health, and benefit human life

clinical trials: studies that determine the effectiveness of new medical treatments or of vaccines

coronavirus: a class of viruses, characterized by surface spike proteins that resemble a crown. Some coronaviruses only affect animals, while others cause cold and flu-like symptoms in humans.

cytoplasm: a jellylike substance that surrounds the nucleus in a living cell. Amino acids, proteins, enzymes, and other organic molecules are found in the cytoplasm.

dendritic cells: special immune cells found in parts of the body that have contact with the outside environment such as the skin or lining of the nose or intestines. Dendritic cells present foreign substances (antigens) to other types of immune cells.

deoxyribonucleic acid (DNA): a self-replicating molecule that contains an organism's genetic material

double-blind study: a type of clinical study in which the participants and the researchers do not know who receives the treatment being tested and who receives a placebo. This reduces the possibility of bias in the results.

enzyme: a substance that increases the rate of a chemical reaction

Human Genome Project: an international research program, from 1990 to 2003, to determine the sequence of nucleotides in human DNA

human immunodeficiency virus (HIV): a virus that seriously impairs the body's immune system and can cause AIDS

immunodeficiency: an inability of the immune system to protect the body from infection or disease

lipid nanoparticle: an extremely small particle of fat that cannot be dissolved in water and that is used to deliver mRNA into cells

lymphocyte: an immune cell found in blood and lymph tissue. The main types are B cells and T cells.

macromolecule: a very large molecule, such as a protein or nucleic acid

messenger RNA (mRNA): the form of RNA that carries protein-making information from the nucleus to the ribosomes in the cytoplasm

metabolism: the chemical activities that maintain life in a body

microbiology: the study of microorganisms, such as bacteria, viruses, parasites, and some fungi

Middle East respiratory syndrome (MERS): a respiratory disease, first identified in Saudi Arabia and caused by a coronavirus

molecule: the smallest particle of a chemical compound with the chemical and physical qualities of that compound

nucleotide: a compound that makes up the structure of nucleic acids, such as DNA

nucleus: an important component of all living cells. Enclosed in a double membrane, the nucleus is essential for all cell activities, including reproduction. It contains the DNA.

protein: a complex substance consisting of chains of amino acids that is present in all living cells. Proteins regulate the metabolism of the cell.

pseudouridine: a nucleotide that is present in transfer RNA. It is used in synthetic mRNA to prevent the inflammatory response.

reagent: a substance used in laboratory tests or chemical analysis

ribonucleic acid (RNA): a nucleic acid found in all living cells. There are three kinds of RNA: messenger RNA (mRNA), transfer RNA (tRNA), and ribosomal RNA (rRNA).

ribosomal RNA (rRNA): RNA that forms the structure of ribosomes along with proteins

severe acute respiratory syndrome (SARS): a severe respiratory disease caused by a coronavirus

T cell: a kind of immune cell circulating in the blood and in lymph tissue. T cells help regulate the immune response and attack tumor cells.

transfer RNA (tRNA): RNA that transfers amino acids necessary for making a protein from the cytoplasm to the ribosomes, where the protein will be made

translation: the process by which coded instructions delivered by mRNA are used to create a protein

vaccine: a substance specially prepared to confer immunity against a disease

virus: a simple microbe that infects cells and causes disease. Viruses can only replicate once they have invaded a cell.

SOURCE NOTES

6 "I feel humbled . . . to help patients.": "University of Pennsylvania mRNA Biology Pioneers Receive COVID-19 Vaccine Enabled by Their Foundational Research," news release, University of Pennsylvania, December 23, 2020, https://www.pennmedicine.org/news/news-releases/2020/december/penn-mrna-biology-pioneers-receive-covid19-vaccine-enabled-by-their-foundational-research#:~:text=December%2023%2C%202020,vaccine%20together%20on%20Friday%2C%20Dec.

11 "You learn so . . . nothing to lose.": Katalin Karikó, interview with the author, January 24, 2023.

15 "I also once . . . a small town.": Mattie Kahn, "The Scientist Who Saved the World," *Glamour*, November 2, 2021, https://www.glamour.com/story/katalin-kariko-biontech-women-of-year-2021.

17 "the happiest years of my life.": "Katalin Karikó, an Alumnus of SZTE Is the Founder of the Most Promising Vaccine Development against the Coronavirus," University of Szeged, April 9, 2020, https://u-szeged.hu/news-and-events/2021/katalin-Kariko-an-alumna.

19 "I knew how . . . not harm anyone.": Boroka Daszkal, "Pfizer's Karikó Was Recruited as an Agent in 1978 by the Socialist Party," *Daily News Hungary*, May 24, 2021, https://dailynewshungary.com/katalin-Kariko-i-didnt-give-any-reports-i-didnt-hurt-anyone/.

22 "So everything was . . . it very exciting.": "Using Chemistry to Enable mRNA Covid-19 Vaccines, Saving Lives and Mitigating the Impacts of the Pandemic: Meet Professor Katalin Karikó," *AND Is the Future*, podcast, episode 8, "Chemistry and Reinventing Progress," accessed March 17, 2023, https://www.solvay.com/en/podcast/chemistry-and-reinventing-progress.

24 "DNA-like RNA": Carolyn Krause, "COVID-19: ORNL's Unsung Discovery of Messenger RNA?," *Oak Ridge (TN) Oakridger*, June 8, 2021, https://www.oakridger.com/story/news/2021/06/09/oak-ridge-tennessee-ornl-scientist-rna-mrna-covid-19-ken-volkin/7600858002/.

25 "I have no . . . way things were.": Krause.

26 "It was more . . . You make it.": Carolyn Johnson, "A One-Way Ticket. A Cash-Stuffed Teddy Bear. A Dream Decades in the Making," *Washington Post*, October 1, 2021, https://www.washingtonpost.com/health/2021/10/01/katalin-kariko-covid-vaccines/.

28 "I can do better than this.": Karikó, interview.

28 "It was going . . . one way trip.": "Katalin Karikó, from Ignored Immigrant to 'Mother' of the Covid-19 Vaccine," archyde.com, January 3, 2021, https://www.archyde.com/katalin-kariko-from-ignored-immigrant-to-mother-of-the-covid-19-vaccine/.

30–31 "When you leave . . . to the surface.": "Hyacinth's message—Katalin Karikó on the Secret of Women's Success," SZTE News, University of Szeged, March 5, 2021, https://u-szeged.hu/sztehirek/2021-marcius/jacintok-uzenete-kariko.

31 "I know how . . . a shoestring budget.": Ian Sample, "Scientists' Egos Are Key Barrier to Progress, Says Covid Vaccine Pioneer," *Guardian* (US edition), September 10, 2021, https://www.theguardian.com/world/2021/sep/10/scientists-egos-key-barrier-to-progress-covid-vaccine-pioneer-katalin-kariko.

34 "You are not . . . to have fun.": Béla Francia, quoted in Gina Kolata, "Kati Karikó Helped Shield the World from the Coronavirus," *New York Times*, updated September 24, 2021, nytimes.com/2021/04/08/health/coronavirus-mrna-kariko.html.

34 "For scientists working . . . could do anything.": David Cox, "How mRNA Went from a Scientific Backwater to a Pandemic Crusher," *Wired*, February 12, 2020, https://www.wired.co.uk/article/mrna-coronavirus-vaccine-pfizer-biontech.

34 "We have to . . . take it there.": David Crow, "How mRNA Became a Vaccine Game-Changer," *FT Magazine*, May 13, 2021, https://www.ft.com/content/b2978026-4bc2-439c-a561-a1972eeba940.

35 "They [officials] thought I would quit.": Katalin Karikó, quoted in Kolata, "Kati Karikó."

36 "You have to . . . to my argument!": Katalin Karikó, quoted in Johnson, "A One-Way Ticket."

36 "Oh my gosh, fantastic!": Béla Francia and Zsuzsanna Francia, quoted in Johnson.

37 "It seems that . . . experiment didn't work.": Katalin Karikó, quoted in Kahn, "The Scientist."

37 "Experiments never err, your expectations do.": Leonardo da Vinci, quoted in Johnson, "A One-Way Ticket."

39 "I was working . . . work with DNA.": Katalin Karikó, quoted in Avis Favaro, Alexandra Mae Jones, and Elizabeth St. Philip, "To Be a Scientist Is a Joy: How a Hungarian Biochemist Helped to Revolutionize mRNA," CTV News, November 14, 2021, https://www.ctvnews.ca/health/to-be-a-scientist-is-a-joy-how-a-hungarian-biochemist-helped-revolutionize-mrna-1.5666043.

39 "I always thought . . . interesting to me.": Katalin Karikó, quoted in Cox, "From a Scientific Backwater to a Pandemic Crusher."

40 "mRNA hustler": Crow, "A Game-Changer."

40 "I'm sorry. I need that money." Katalin Karikó, interview with Michael Barbaro, host, "The Unlikely Pioneer behind mRNA Vaccines," *New York Times*, June 19, 2021, transcript of the podcast, https://www.nytimes.com/2021/06/10/podcasts/the-daily/mrna-vaccines-katalin-kariko.html?showTranscript=1.

41 "faculty material": Dana Kennedy, "This Scientist's Decades of mRNA Research Led to Both COVID-19 Vaccines," *New York Post*, December 5, 2020, https://nypost.com/2020/12/05/this-scientists-decades-of-mrna-research-led-to-covid-vaccines/.

41 "Kati works for me.": Johnson, "A One-Way Ticket."

41 "I don't work . . . and to understand.": Katalin Karikó, quoted in Johnson.

42 "I am an . . . anything with mRNA.": Katalin Karikó, quoted in Kolata, "Kati Karikó."

43 "If you make . . . I'll try it.": Andrew Weissman, quoted in Gregory Zuckerman, *A Shot to Save the World: The Inside Story of the Life-or-Death Race for a Covid-19 Vaccine* (London: Portfolio, Penguin, 2021), 66.

43 "I am the . . . educated each other.": Katalin Karikó, quoted in Crow, "A Game-Changer."

45 "The person who . . . didn't give up.": Andrew Weissman, quoted in Carolyn Y. Johnson, "A Scientific Hunch. Then Silence. Until the World Needed a Lifesaving Vaccine," *Washington Post*, October 1, 2021, https://www.washingtonpost.com/science/2021/10/01/drew-weissman-mrna-vaccine/.

49 "I had spent . . . it was useless.": Katalin Karikó, interview with Ushma S. Neill, "A Conversation with Katalin Karikó," *Journal of Clinical Investigation*, November 1, 2021, https://www.jci.org/articles/view/155559.

51 "Oh my God . . . can use it.": Katalin Karikó, quoted in Crow, "A Game-Changer."

52 "Our phones are . . . off the hook.": Andrew Weissman, quoted in Ting Yu, "How Scientists Drew Weissman and Katalin Karikó Developed the Revolutionary mRNA Technology inside COVID Vaccines," *Bostonia*, November 18, 2021, https://www.bu.edu/articles/2021/how-drew-weissman-and-katalin-Kariko-developed-mrna-technology-inside-covid-vaccines/.

54 "This is unbelievable.": Andrew Weissman, quoted in Zuckerman, *A Shot to Save the World*, 80.

55 "What's it good for?": Crow, "A Game-Changer."

55 "You know what . . . for growing hair.": Katalin Karikó, quoted in Crow.

55 "Really?": Crow.

55 "Yes, it could be.": Katalin Karikó, quoted in Crow.

56 "We didn't want . . . about the money.": Nancy Ruhling, Susan Polgar, and Gabriel Erem, "The Incredible (Scientific) Journey of Prof. Karikó," *Lifestyles Magazine*, pre-spring 2021, https://lifestylesmagazine.com/profile/katalin-Kariko/.

56 "They just asked for too much.": Andrew Weissman, quoted in Zuckerman, *A Shot to Save the World*, 82.

57 "She always said . . . was driving her.": Katalin Karikó, quoted in Julia Kollewe, "Covid Vaccine Technology Pioneer: I Never Doubted It Would Work," *Guardian* (US edition), November 1, 2020, https://www.theguardian.com/science/2020/nov/21/covid-vaccine-technology-pioneer-i-never-doubted-it-would-work.

57 "My mother said . . . my family proud.": Susan Francia, "The Best Cheerleader," Team USA, June 17, 2011, https://www.teamusa.org/Bloggers-for-TeamUSA/Susan-Francia/The-Best-Cheerleader.

58 "required a trust . . . out that way.": Susan Francia, "Olympian Susan Francia on How Her Mother Helped Develop the COVID-19 Vaccines and Their American Dream," with Tonya Simpson, *ESPN*, July 28, 2021, https://www.espn.com/olympics/story/_/id/31707795/olympian-susan-francia-how-mother-helped-develop-covid-19-vaccines-their-american-dream.

60 "adding an entirely . . . the pharmaceutical arsenal": Damian Garde and Jonathan Saltzman, "The Story of mRNA: How a Once-Dismissed Idea Became a Leading Technology in the Covid Vaccine Race," Stat, November 10, 2020, https://www.statnews.com/2020/11/10/the-story-of-mrna-how-a-once-dismissed-idea-became-a-leading-technology-in-the-covid-vaccine-race/.

61 "earned through hard work": Philip Oltermann, "Uğur Şahin and Özlem Türeci: German 'Dream Team' behind Vaccine," *Guardian* (US edition), November 10, 2020, https://www.theguardian.com/world/2020/nov/10/ugur-sahin-and-ozlem-tureci-german-dream-team-behind-vaccine.

62 "We need you,": Uğur Şahin, quoted in Brendan Borrell, *The First Shots: The Epic Rivalries and Heroic Science behind the Race to the Coronavirus Vaccine* (Boston: Mariner Books, 2021), 109.

63 "BioNTech doesn't even have a website.": Katalin Karikó, quoted in Cox, "From a Scientific Backwater to a Pandemic Crusher."

64 "In my first . . . missed my family.": Katalin Karikó, quoted in Ruhling, Polgar, and Erem, "The Incredible (Scientific) Journey."

65 "We [BioNTech] have . . . nobody would read.": Katalin Karikó, quoted in Claudia Lopez Lloreda, "Messenger RNA Vaccine Pioneer Katalin Karikó Shares Her Long Journey to Covid-19 Vaccines," Stat, July 19, 2021, https://www.statnews.com/2021/07/19/katalin-Kariko-messenger-rna-vaccine-pioneer/.

65 "key challenges and . . . class of drugs": Uğur Şahin, Katalin Karikó, and Özlem Türeci, "mRNA-Based Therapeutics—Developing a New Class of Drugs," *Nature Reviews Drug Discovery*, September 14, 2014, https://www.researchgate.net/publication/265861982_mRNA-based_therapeitics-Developing_a_new_class_of_drugs.

69 "He's a visionary . . . something with that.'": Katalin Karikó, quoted in Matthew De George, "The Vaccine Trenches," *Pennsylvania Gazette*, April 20, 2021, https://thepenngazette.com/the-vaccine-trenches/.

73 "It's all a . . . hundreds of people.": Pieter Cullis, quoted in Kerry Banks, "This Canadian Scientist Helped Lay the Groundwork for Pandemic-Taming COVID-19 Vaccines," *University Affairs*, May 18, 2022, https://www.universityaffairs.ca/features/feature-article/this-canadian-scientist-helped-lay-the-groundwork-for-pandemic-taming-covid-19-vaccines/#:~:text=Paul%20Joseph%2FUBC.-,This%20Canadian%20scientist%20helped%20lay%20the%20groundwork%20for%20pandemic%2Dtaming,system'%20used%20in%20mRNA%20technology.

75 "Any vaccine can . . . a few days.": "Possible Side Effects from Vaccines," CDC, last updated April 20, 2020, https://www.cdc.gov/vaccines/vac-gen/side-effects.htm.

77 "We need to . . . is our time.": Barney Graham, quoted in Gina Kolata and Benjamin Mueller, "Halting Progress and Happy Accidents: How mRNA Vaccines Were Made," *New York Times*, January 15, 2022, https://www.nytimes.com/2022/01/15/health/mrna-vaccine.html.

78 "I think we . . . have to contribute.": Uğur Şahin, quoted in Zuckerman, *A Shot to Save the World*, 246.

79 "From 2018 we . . . a technical thing.": Katalin Karikó, quoted in Tanya Lewis, "An mRNA Pioneer Discusses How Her Work Led to the COVID Vaccines," *Scientific American*, September 15, 2021, https://www.scientificamerican.com/article/an-mrna-pioneer-discusses-how-her-work-led-to-the-covid-vaccines/.

79 "I was aware . . . an excellent vaccine.": Katalin Karikó, quoted in Lewis.

80 "It took us . . . was very dangerous.": Zhang Yongzhen, quoted in Charlie Campbell, "Exclusive: The Chinese Scientist Who Sequenced the First COVID-19 Genome Speaks Out about the Controversies Surrounding His Work," *Time*, August 24, 2020, https://time.com/5882918/zhang-yongzhen-interview-china-coronavirus-genome/.

80 "Can you release . . . it to me." Eddie Holmes, quoted in Zuckerman, *A Shot to Save the World*, 235.

81 "I asked Eddie . . . I said ok.": Zhang Yongzhen, quoted in Campbell, "Exclusive."

81 "outstanding data sharing": Brendan Borrell, *The First Shots*, 264.

88 "People are feeling . . . to an end.": Francis Collins, quoted in "Dr. Anthony Fauci on COVID-19 Vaccines," *NIH News in Health*, August 2020, https://newsinhealth.nih.gov/2020/08/dr-anthony-fauci-covid-19-vaccines.

88 "the scientific voice of reason": Jon Cohen, "I'm Going to Keep Pushing Anthony Fauci to Make the White House Listen to Facts of the Pandemic," *Science*, March 22, 2020, https://www.science.org/content/article/i-m-going-keep-pushing-anthony-fauci-tries-make-white-house-listen-facts-pandemic.

88 "The uncertainty and . . . get through this?": Francis Collins, quoted in "Dr. Anthony Fauci," *NIH News in Health*.

89 "aimed to produce . . . by January 2021.": "Operation Warp Speed: Accelerated COVID-19 Vaccine Development Status and Efforts to Address Manufacturing Challenges," GAO, February 11, 2021, https://www.gao.gov/products/gao-21-319.

89 "[Operation Warp Speed] . . . the pandemic response.": Jesse Goodman, quoted in Mark Gollom, "Why Trump's Operation Warp Speed Is Credited with Helping Race for COVID-19 Vaccine," CBC News, November 19, 2020, https://www.cbc.ca/news/health/operation-warp-speed-trump-pfizer-moderna-vaccine-1.5806820.

89 "You can like . . . success, unprecedented success.": Tinglong Dai, quoted in Gollom.

90 "We will get . . . we promise you.": Anthony Fauci, quoted in "Dr. Anthony Fauci."

90 "Watch the news . . . Google search: BioNTech.": Katalin Karikó, quoted in Johnson, "A Scientific Hunch."

91 "I started to . . . dying or something." Katalin Karikó, quoted in "Katalin Karikó, from Ignored Immigrant to 'Mother' of the Covid-19 Vaccine," *NewsBeezer*, January 3, 2021, https://newsbeezer.com/chileeng/katalin-Kariko-from-ignored-immigrant-to-mother-of-the-covid-19-vaccine/.

91 "Oh, it works. . . . knew it would.": Katalin Karikó, interview with Michael Barbero, "The Unlikely Pioneer behind mRNA Vaccines," *New York Times*, June 10, 2021, transcript, https://www.nytimes.com/2021/06/10/podcasts/the-daily/mrna-vaccines-katalin-kariko.html?showTranscript=1.

91 "Today I'm going . . . the whole [box].": Karikó, interview with Barbero.

93 "a revolution in American medicine": Michael Specter, "How Anthony Fauci Became America's Doctor," *New Yorker*, April 10, 2020, https://www.newyorker.com/magazine/2020/04/20/how-anthony-fauci-became-americas-doctor.

93 "You stay completely . . . And that's it.": Anthony Fauci, quoted in Specter.

94 "Today is a . . . science and humanity.": Anthony Bourla, quoted in "Pfizer and BioNTech Announce Candidate against COVID-19 Achieved Success in First Interim Analysis from Phase 3 Study," Pfizer, press release, November 9, 2020, https://www.pfizer.com/news/press-release/press-release-detail/pfizer-and-biontech-announce-vaccine-candidate-against.

94 "When we embarked . . . sense of normality.": Uğur Şahin, quoted in "Pfizer and BioNTech."

94–95 "the known and . . . of the vaccine.": "Emergency Use Authorization for Vaccines Explained," US Food and Drug Administration, last modified November 11, 2020, https://www.fda.gov/vaccines-blood-biologics/vaccines/emergency-use-authorization-vaccines-explained.

95 "I'm hopeful now . . . other diseases too.": Katalin Karikó, quoted in "University of Pennsylvania mRNA Pioneers Receive COVID-19 Vaccine Enabled by Their Foundational Research," Penn Medicine News, press release, December 23, 2020, https://www.pennmedicine.org/news/news-releases/2020/december/penn-mrna-biology-pioneers-receive-covid19-vaccine-enabled-by-their-foundational-research.

95 "quirky . . . cheerful": Kennedy, "This Scientist's Decades of mRNA Research."

96 "I was like . . . shivers, no fears.": Sandra Lindsay, quoted in Peter D. Kramer, "Historic Jab; Meet Sandra Lindsay, the First COVID-19 Vaccine Recipient in the U.S.," *Rockland/Westchester (NY) Journal News*, updated March 14, 2022, https://www.lohud.com/in-depth/opinion/2022/03/13/sandra-lindsay-new-york-usa-today-women-of-the-year/9298622002/.

96 "inspire people who . . . about taking vaccines": Sandra Lindsay, quoted in Sharon Otterman, "'I Trust Science,' Says Nurse Who Is First to Get Vaccine in U.S.," *New York Times*, updated December 17, 2020, https://www.nytimes.com/2020/12/14/nyregion/us-covid-vaccine-first-sandra-lindsay.html.

97 "I just felt . . . loss of livelihoods": Sandra Lindsay, quoted in the Associated Press, "First COVID-19 Shot Recipient in US Now a Vaccine Activist," nbcnews.com, December 28, 2021, https://www.nbcnews.com/news/us-news/first-covid-shot-recipient-us-now-vaccine-activist-rcna10167.

98 "I like what . . . Nothing will change.": Katalin Karikó, quoted in Kennedy, "This Scientist's Decades of mRNA Research."

98 "People's concerns need . . . professionals they trust.": Karikó, quoted in Ruhling, Polgar, and Erem, "The Incredible (Scientific) Journey."

100 "threatens to reverse . . . tackling vaccine-preventable diseases.": Megan Trimble, "WHO: Anti-Vaccine Movement a Top Threat in 2019," *U.S. News & World Report*, January 16, 2019, https://www.usnews.com/news/national-news/articles/2019-01-16/who-names-vaccine-hesitancy-as-top-world-threat-in-2019.

100 "pandemic of the unvaccinated": Brian Myers, "Opinion: The False 'Pandemic of the Unvaccinated' Motto Did Lasting Harm," *Des Moines Register*, April 17, 2022, https://www.desmoinesregister.com/story/opinion/columnists/iowa-view/2022/04/17/covid-pandemic-unvaccinated-motto-false-lasting-harm/7320097001/.

100 "People who are . . . of the unvaccinated.": Günter Kampf, "COVID-19: Stigmatizing the Unvaccinated Is Not Justified," *Lancet*, November 20, 2021, https://www.thelancet.com/pdfs/journals/lancet/PIIS0140-6736(21)02243-1.pdf.

101 "Addressing health misinformation . . . seen with COVID.": Vivek Hallegere Murthy, quoted in Erika Edwards, "A Threat to the Next Pandemic: Vaccine Hesitancy," NBC News, May 2, 2022, https://www.nbcnews.com/health/health-news/major-threat-pandemic-vaccine-hesitancy-rcna25460.

101 "We know that . . . a different place.": Greta Massetti, quoted in Emily Anthes, "CDC Eases Covid Guidelines, Noting 'Virus Is Here to Stay,'" *New York Times*, August 11, 2022, https://www.nytimes.com/2022/08/11/health/virus-cdc-guidelines.html.

102 "I want to . . . patients with cancer": Katalin Karikó, quoted in Philip Andrew Churm, "Biochemist Karikó Honoured in Her Hungarian Home Town for COVID Work," Euronews, May 22, 2021, https://www.euronews.com/2021/05/22/biochemist-kariko-honoured-in-her-hungarian-home-town-for-covid-work.

102 "How about we . . . in the fridge?": Katalin Karikó, quoted in Kollewe, "Covid Vaccine Technology Pioneer."

103 "There's no question . . . as they can": Karikó, quoted in Ruhling, Polgar, and Erem, "The Incredible (Scientific) Journey."

105 "I never sought . . . without any prize": Katalin Karikó, quoted in Tom Avril, "Penn Scientists Win $3 million Breakthrough Prize for RNA Research That Enabled COVID-19 Vaccines," *Philadelphia Inquirer*, September 9, 2021, https://www.inquirer.com/health/coronavirus/kariko-weissman-breakthrough-prize-covid19-vaccine-biontech-20210909.html.

105 "When you see . . . kind of feeling": Katalin Karikó, quoted in Neill, "A Conversation with Katalin Karikó."

106 "I was curious": Katalin Karikó, "Humanitas University, Opening of the Academic 2021/22 Year. Katalin Karikó Accepting the Honorary Degree," University of Szeged, November 29, 2021, https://u-szeged.hu/download.php?docID=124639.

106 "We spend most . . . to enjoy it": Karikó, "Humanitas University."

106 "parents who taught . . . part of life.": Karikó, "Humanitas University."

108 "I just love . . . work bear fruit.": Katalin Karikó, quoted in Kennedy, "This Scientist's Decades of mRNA Research."

108 "They were all . . . is a winner": Katalin Karikó, interview with the author.

108 "The science has . . . be the goal": Karikó.

109 "because without them . . . be so tough.": Karikó.

113 "The worst thing . . . to worry about.": Tedros Adhanom Ghebreyesus, quoted in Alexander Tin, "COVID Global Health Emergency Is Officially Ending, WHO Says, but Warns Virus Remains a Risk," CBS News, May 5, 2023, https://www.cbsnews.com/news/who-covid-emergency-world-health-organization/.

SELECTED BIBLIOGRAPHY

Anita, Elo. "'Karikó's Assertion Cannot Be Refuted'—The Director General of the Historical Archives of the State Security Services about the Agent Accusation." Válasz Online, May 23, 2021. https://www.valaszonline.hu/2021/05/23/Karikos-assertion-cannot-be-refuted/.

Ball, Philip. "The Lightning-Fast Quest for COVID Vaccines—And What It Means for Other Diseases." *Nature*, December 18, 2020. https://www.nature.com/articles/d41586-020-03626-1.

Barbaro, Michael. "The Unlikely Pioneer behind mRNA Vaccines." Produced by Rachel Quester, Jessica Cheung, and Robert Szypko. *New York Times* podcast. Transcript, June 10, 2021. https://www.nytimes.com/2021/06/10/podcasts/the-daily/mrna-vaccines-katalin-kariko.html.

Borrell, Brendan. *The First Shots: The Epic Rivalries and Heroic Science behind the Race to the Coronavirus Vaccine*. Boston: Mariner Books, 2021.

Bourla, Albert. *Moonshot: Inside Pfizer's Nine-Month Race to Make the Impossible Possible*. New York: Harper Business, 2022.

"COVID-19: ORNL's Unsung Discovery of Messenger RNA." *Oak Ridge (TN) Oakridger*, June 8, 2021. https://www.oakridger.com/story/news/2021/06/09/oak-ridge-tennessee-ornl-scientist-rna-mrna-covid-19-ken-volkin/7600858002/.

Cox, David. "How mRNA Went from a Scientific Backwater to a Pandemic Crusher." *Wired*, December 2, 2020. https://www.wired.co.uk/article/mrna-coronavirus-vaccine-pfizer-biontech.

Crow, David. "How mRNA Became a Vaccine Game-Changer." *FT Magazine*, May 13, 2021. https://www.ft.com/content/b2978026-4bc2-439c-a561-a1972eeba940.

Crowcroft, Orlando. "'I Was Innocent': Soviet-Era Ghosts Return to Haunt COVID-19 Vaccine Scientist." Euronews. Updated May 27, 2021. https://www.euronews.com/my-europe/2021/05/25/i-was-innocent-soviet-era-ghosts-return-to-haunt-covid-19-vaccine-scientist.

Edwards, Kathryn M., Walter Orenstein, and David S. Stephens. *The Covid-19 Vaccine Guide: The Quest for Implementation of Safe and Effective Vaccinations*. New York: Skyhorse, 2021.

Francia, Susan. "Olympian Susan Francia on How Her Mother Helped Develop the COVID-19 Vaccines and Their American Dream." With Tonya Simpson. *ESPN*, June 28, 2021. https://www.espn.com/olympics/story/_/id/31707795/olympian-susan-francia-how-mother-helped-develop-covid-19-vaccines-their-american-dream.

Frangou, Christina. "Researchers Looking for mRNA Were Ridiculed by Colleagues. Luckily, That Didn't Stop Them." *MacLean's*, February 18, 2021. https://macleans.ca/society/science/scientists-mrna-covid-vaccines/.

Gallagher, Paul. "Katalin Karikó: Covid-19 Vaccine Pioneer Urges More Girls and Young Women to Take Up Science." Inews.co.uk, February 15, 2022. https://inews.co.uk/news/science/katalin-kariko-covid-19-vaccine-pioneer-urges-more-girls-and-young-women-to-take-up-science-1460380.

Garde, Damian, and Jonathan Saltzman. "The Story of mRNA: How a Once-Dismissed Idea Became a Leading Technology in the Covid Vaccine Race." Stat, November 10, 2020. https://www.statnews.com/2020/11/10/the-story-of-mrna-how-a-once-dismissed-idea-became-a-leading-technology-in-the-covid-vaccine-race/.

Gates, Bill. "She Helped Change Vaccines Forever." *Gates Notes: The Blog of Bill Gates*, April 30, 2022. https://www.gatesnotes.com/Health/Heroes-in-the-field-Katalin-Kariko.

Isaacson, Walter. "mRNA Technology Gave Us the First COVID-19 Vaccines. It Could Also Upend the Drug Industry." *Time*, January 11, 2021. https://time.com/5927342/mrna-covid-vaccine/.

Johnson, Carolyn Y. "A One-Way Ticket. A Cash-Stuffed Teddy Bear. A Dream Decades in the Making." *Washington Post*, October 1, 2021. https://www.washingtonpost.com/health/2021/10/01/katalin-kariko-covid-vaccines/.

Johnson, Steven. *Extra Life: A Short History of Living Longer*. New York: Riverhead Books, 2021.

Kahn, Mattie. "Women of the Year: The Scientist Who Saved the World." *Glamour*, November 2, 2021. https://www.glamour.com/story/katalin-kariko-biontech-women-of-year-2021.

Karikó, Katalin. "Humanitas University, Opening of the Academic 2021/22 Year. Katalin Karikó, Accepting the Honorary Degree." University of Szeged, November 29, 2021. https://u-szeged.hu/download.php?docID=124639.

———. Phone interview with the author, January 24, 2023.

Karikó, Katalin, Hiromi Muramatsu, Frank A. Walsh, Janos Ludwig, Hiroki Kato, Shizuo Akira, and Drew Weissman. "Incorporation of Pseudouridine into mRNA Yields Superior Nonimmunogenic Vector with Increased Translational Capacity and Biological Stability." *Molecular Therapy* 16, no. 11 (November 2008): 1833–1840. doi:10.1038/mt.2008.200.

Karikó, Katalin, Michael Buckstein, Houping Ni, and Drew Weissman. "Suppression of RNA Recognition by Toll-Like Receptors: The Impact of Nucleoside Modification and the Evolutionary Origin of RNA." *Immunity* 23 (August 2005): 165–175.

"Katalin Karikó, a Former Excellent Student of the University of Szeged, an Honorary Citizen of the City Szeged." Virtual exhibit. University of Szeged Klebelsberg Kuno Library, 2021. Translated. https://mediateka.ek.szte.hu/exhibits/show/Kariko_katalin_szte/bevezeto.

Kennedy, Dana. "This Scientist's Decades of mRNA Research Led to Both COVID-19 Vaccines." *New York Post*. Updated December 5, 2020. https://nypost.com/2020/12/05/this-scientists-decades-of-mrna-research-led-to-covid-vaccines/.

Kolata, Gina. "How Did the Inventor of mRNA Vaccines Celebrate Her Success? She Ate a Whole Bag of Goobers." *Irish Times*, August 17, 2021. https://www.irishtimes.com/life-and-style/health-family/how-did-the-inventor-of-mrna-vaccines-celebrate-her-success-she-ate-a-whole-bag-of-goobers-1.4648542.

———."Kati Karikó Helped Shield the World from the Coronavirus." *New York Times*, April 8, 2021. https://www.nytimes.com/2021/04/08/health/coronavirus-mrna-kariko.html.

Kollewe, Julia. "Covid Vaccine Technology Pioneer: 'I Never Doubted It Would Work.'" *Guardian* (US edition), November 21, 2021. https://www.theguardian.com/science/2020/nov/21/covid-vaccine-technology-pioneer-i-never-doubted-it-would-work.

Lewis, Tanya. "An mRNA Pioneer Discusses How Her Work Led to the COVID Vaccines." *Scientific American*, September 15, 2021. https://www.scientificamerican.com/article/an-mrna-pioneer-discusses-how-her-work-led-to-the-covid-vaccines/.

Lloreda, Claudia Lopez. "Messenger RNA Vaccine Pioneer Katalin Karikó Shares Her Long Journey to Covid-19 Vaccines." Stat, July 19, 2021. https://www.statnews.com/2021/07/19/katalin-Kariko-messenger-rna-vaccine-pioneer/.

MacKenzie, Debora. *COVID-19: The Pandemic That Never Should Have Happened*. New York: Hachette Books, 2020.

Miller, Joe. *The Vaccine: Inside the Race to Conquer the COVID-19 Pandemic*. With Özlem Türeci and Uğur Şahin. New York: St. Martin's, 2022.

Nair, Prashant. "QnAs with Katalin Karikó." *PNAS* 118, no. 51 (December 13, 2021). https://www.pnas.org/doi/10.1073/pnas.2119757118.

Newey, Sarah, and Paul Nuki. "'Redemption': How a Scientist's Unwavering Belief in mRNA Gave the World a Covid-19 Vaccine." *Telegraph* (London), December 2, 2020. https://www.telegraph.co.uk/global-health/science-and-disease/redemption-one-scientists-unwavering-belief-mrna-gave-world/.

Ruhling, Nancy, Susan Polgar, and Gabriel Erem. "The Incredible (Scientific) Journey of Prof. Karikó." *Lifestyles Magazine*, pre-spring 2021. http://www.lifestylesmagazine.com/web/wp-content/uploads/2021/02/Kariko.pdf.

Thompson, Derek. "How mRNA Technology Could Change the World." *Atlantic*, March 29, 2021. https://www.theatlantic.com/ideas/archive/2021/03/how-mrna-technology-could-change-world/618431/.

Vaski, Tomas. "Katalin Karikó's Elementary Biology Teacher: We Knew She Was Gifted." Hungary Today, June 12, 2021. Translated. https://hungarytoday.hu/katalin-Kariko-origin-biology-teacher-hungary/.

———. "Pfizer-BioNTech Vaccine Creator Karikó: Research Is My Passion, I'm Not a Hero, Healthcare Workers Are the Heroes." Hungary Today, May 12, 2021. Translated. https://hungarytoday.hu/katalin-Kariko-zoran-inspiration-pfizer-biontech-vaccine-creator-klubradio/.

Zuckerman, Gregory. *A Shot to Save the World: The Inside Story of the Life-or-Death Race for a Covid-19 Vaccine*. London: Portfolio Penguin, 2021.

FURTHER INFORMATION

Books

Brown, Don. *A Shot in the Arm!* New York: Harry N. Abrams, 2021.
Learn more about the development of vaccines from the first smallpox inoculations in the late eighteenth century to the COVID-19 vaccines in this graphic novel.

Haelle, Tara. *Vaccination Investigation: The History and Science of Vaccines.* Minneapolis: Twenty-First Century Books, 2018.
Written before the COVID-19 pandemic, this book provides a thorough and fascinating account of the development of vaccines and includes material on herd immunity, the antivaccination movement, and the threat climate change poses to the spread of diseases.

Ibura, Ki. *When the World Turned Upside Down.* New York: Scholastic, 2022.
In this middle-grade novel, students respond to the coronavirus pandemic by trying to help their neighbors and their community.

King-Cargile, Gillian. *Vaccines Change the World.* Park Ridge, IL: Albert Whitman, 2022.
This book discusses pandemics and presents stories about vaccines and the people who developed them.

Messner, Kate. *History Smashers: Plagues and Pandemics.* New York: Random House, 2021.
COVID-19 wasn't the first pandemic. Check out this book to learn more about historic deadly diseases, starting with the bubonic plague.

Polinsky, Paige V. *Vaccines: A Graphic History.* Minneapolis: Graphic Universe, 2022.
Gain more understanding of the development of vaccines with this visual depiction of how scientists make them.

Walters, Eric. *Don't Stand So Close to Me.* Olympia, WA: Orca Books, 2020.
In this middle-grade novel, the lives of thirteen-year-old Quinn and her friends change dramatically as their school goes online and social distancing measures are enacted during the pandemic.

Videos

The First Wave. Directed by Matthew Heineman. Produced by Matthew Heineman, Jenna Millman, and Leslie Norville. National Geographic Documentary Films, 2021.

Watch how the heroic staff of a New York hospital dealt with the hardships of the first four months of the COVID-19 pandemic.

How to Survive a Pandemic. Directed by David France. Produced by Mira Chang. Impact Partners, Sandbox Films, and Public Square Films, 2022.

This film documents the development, manufacture, and distribution of the COVID-19 vaccine.

In the Same Breath. Directed and produced by Nanfu Wang. HBO Documentary Films. 2021.

This well-regarded film compares how the governments of China and the United States each reacted to the coronavirus pandemic.

"Katalin Karikó and Drew Weissman Awarded Horwitz Prize for Pioneering Research on COVID-19 Vaccines." YouTube video. Posted by Columbia University Irving Medical Center. https://www.youtube.com/watch?v=H7BgkEcgUxg.

Hear from Karikó and Weissman in this interview after they received the Horwitz Prize, an award for groundbreaking medical science given yearly by Columbia University.

The Shot. Onza and BioInnova with GSK. Amazon Prime, November 14, 2022.

Covering the last fifty years of vaccine history, this documentary includes first-person accounts from noted scientists in the field, including Katalin Karikó.

Websites

BioNTech

https://www.biontech.com/int/en/home.html

Besides providing general information on the company, BioNTech's website on mRNA discusses therapies, antibodies, clinical trials, and other topics.

CDC COVID-19

https://www.cdc.gov/coronavirus/2019-ncov/variants/about-variants.html

This website from the CDC discusses variants of the coronavirus and how they are monitored.

NIH: Our Science and the Covid-19 Pandemic—Katalin Karikó's Research Idea and Her Perseverance
https://www.ncbi.nlm.nih.gov/pmc/articles/PMC8143802/
Check out some of the diagrams and pictures provided by Karikó to this brief biography of her life and work, created by two professors from Budapest University of Technology and Economics.

Penn Medicine: Katalin Karikó, PhD
https://www.pennmedicine.org/providers/profile/katalin-Kariko
Katalin Karikó's profile page from the University of Pennsylvania contains links related to her work and to the vaccine, including one to her 2005 groundbreaking paper with Drew Weissman.

The Power of mRNA
https://www.modernatx.com/power-of-mrna/science-of-mrna
Learn the basic facts about proteins and mRNA from pharmaceutical company Moderna.

INDEX

ACKNOWLEDGMENTS

I would like to express my deep gratitude to Dr. Katalin Karikó for generously sharing her time and memories. Thanks also to my editor Oliver Katz for his guidance and insights, to editors Shaina Olmanson and Jesseca Fusco for their support and help, and to my husband Richard for his constant encouragement and help with biological concepts.

ABOUT THE AUTHOR

Stephanie Sammartino McPherson wrote her first children's story in college. She enjoyed the process so much that she's never stopped writing. A former teacher and freelance newspaper writer, she has written more than thirty books and numerous magazine stories. Her recent books include *The Global Refugee Crisis: Fleeing Conflict and Violence* and *Hothouse Earth: The Climate Crisis and the Importance of Carbon Neutrality*, winner of the Green Earth Book Award for young adult nonfiction. Stephanie and her husband, Richard, live in Virginia.

PHOTO ACKNOWLEDGMENTS

Image credits: Scott Heins/Getty Images, p. 5; Photos provided by Dr. Katalin Karikó and her daughter, Zsuzsanna (Susan) Francia, pp. 9, 13, 16, 19, 28, 29, 33, 44, 45, 53, 57, 62; Mario De Biasi\Archivio Mario De Biasi\Mondadori/Getty Images, p. 10; Bettmann Archive/Getty Images, pp. 15, 70; Cambridge News/Mirrorpix/Getty Images, p. 25; MShieldsPhotos/Alamy, p. 32; Aldona Griskeviciene/Shutterstock, p. 38; VectorMine/Shutterstock, p. 47; Imagebroker/Alamy, p. 48; DjMiko/iStock/Getty Images, p. 49; Courtesy of National Human Genome Research Institute or NHGRI, p. 54; AP Photo/Kevork Djansezian, p. 58; AP Photo/Bernd von Jutrczenka/picture-alliance/dpa, p. 61; Juancho Torres/Anadolu Agency/Getty Images, p. 66; AUGUSTIN WAMENYA/AFP/Getty Images, p. 72; Science Photo Library RF/agency/Getty Images, p. 76; Noel Celis/Pool via REUTERS/Alamy, p. 81; Nic Coury/Bloomberg/Getty Images, p. 83; Juanmonino/E+/Getty Images, p. 88; Peter Ansin/Mikki Ansin/Getty Images, p. 92; Shannon Stapleton-Pool/Getty Images, p. 96; Kyodo News/Getty Images, p. 105; Andriy Onufriyenko/Getty Images, p. 107; Backgrounds: Yuichiro Chino/Moment/Getty Images.

Cover: Yuichiro Chino/Moment/Getty Images; Peter Stark/fStop/Getty Images.